4.00
100k

Women's Studies in the United States

by Catharine R. Stimpson
with Nina Kressner Cobb

305.42
S 85

A REPORT TO THE FORD FOUNDATION

One of a series of reports on activities supported by the Ford Foundation. A complete
list of publications may be obtained from
the Ford Foundation, Office of Reports,
320 East 43 Street, New York, N.Y. 10017.

**Library of Congress Cataloging-in-
Publication Data**
Stimpson, Catharine R.
   Women's studies in the United States.

   Bibliography: p.
   1. Women's studies—United States.
2. Women—Study and teaching—United
States.   I. Cobb, Nina Kressner.   II. Ford
Foundation.   III. Title.
HQ1181.U5S75   1986   305.4'2'0973
86-9867   ISBN 0-916584-26-7

Contents

Foreword

In 1972 the Ford Foundation began a program to promote the advancement of women and help eliminate sex discrimination in all phases of education. The aims of the program were to encourage research by and about women, to revise school and college curricula to give more attention to the role of women, to increase women's opportunities in certain professions and in positions of educational leadership, and to monitor enforcement of sex-bias laws in educational institutions. By 1979 more than $9 million had been granted to address these various concerns. In 1980 the Foundation's Board of Trustees more than doubled previous Foundation allocations for women's programs. The aim was to expand the most promising of the earlier programs and to explore new activities on behalf of women.*

Early on, the Foundation recognized that the key to correcting many sex-related inequalities is a better understanding of the development and significance of sex differences and, more broadly, of the role of women in society. This recognition led in 1972 to the creation of the first

---

* Two accounts of early Foundation programs are *That 51 Percent: Ford Foundation Activities Related to Opportunities for Women* (1974) and *That 51 Percent Plus* (1979), both available free of charge.

national program of faculty and doctoral dissertation fellowships for research on the role of women. The fellowships were followed by a series of grants establishing centers for research on women at leading colleges and universities throughout the country, including Stanford, the University of California (Berkeley), Wellesley, Brown, Duke, and the University of Arizona. In encouraging institutional support for women's studies, the Foundation was signaling a long-term commitment to this emerging field of scholarly inquiry.

Since 1980 the Foundation has supported projects that have taken on such challenges as how to get the results of women's studies research into the hands of policy makers and how that research should affect the liberal arts curriculum. As our work proceeded, we saw a need for an outside review that would assess the Foundation's efforts in women's studies and place them in a broader context. We asked Catharine R. Stimpson, professor of literature at Rutgers University, to undertake this task. Later, we called upon Nina Kressner Cobb, an editor who has specialized in women's studies, to help prepare the report for publication.

As founding editor of the highly regarded *Signs: Journal of Women in Culture and Society,* Catharine Stimpson has, for over a decade, been at the center of the intellectual ferment created by the new scholarship on women. She currently heads Rutgers' Women's Studies Program and chairs the board of the National Council for Research on Women, an organization representing nearly fifty centers that conduct scholarly work on women's roles and contributions to society. In her various capacities Professor Stimpson has been able to deepen her knowledge of the current state of women's studies research, curriculum development, and outreach to policy makers, not only in the United States but in other countries as well.

This broad vision informs the present report. By tying the development of women's studies to other efforts to reform higher education, as well as to the wider women's movement, she reminds us that the new scholarship emerges not only from the concerns of the academy but also from a societal need to treat women differently. In its discussion of the current debate among women's studies scholars over whether social conditioning is the basis for gender differences, the report reflects the intellectual vitality and diversity characteristic of the best of the new scholarship on women. There is no single "feminist" ideology that women's studies scholars must adopt. Indeed, there are multiple theories to explain the differences between men and women and their roles in society. Finally, the report's observations on the future of women's studies provide recommendations for broadening the research effort, consolidating the gains made, and strengthening existing institutions. In short, the report reveals, a great deal has been done in the past fifteen years, but more work remains.

We think Professor Stimpson's report offers valuable insights into the development of women's studies in the United States, and we are pleased to publish it. We hope that it will stimulate further discussion among donors and scholars about ways to maintain and build upon an already impressive achievement.

SUSAN V. BERRESFORD
Vice President, United States and
International Affairs Programs
Ford Foundation

Preface and Acknowledgments

This is an essay on women's studies in higher education in the United States. It began in 1982 as a consultant's report to the Ford Foundation. Since revised, edited, and shortened for publication, its purpose is no longer to make suggestions to a philanthropic organization but to present to a general audience a view of women's studies as it exists today. The remaining occasional references to the Foundation reflect both the essay's origins and the long and continuing role played by the Foundation in women's studies.

I am grateful to the many colleagues, friends, and acquaintances who have shared with me their views of women's studies over the years. I am also indebted to the people to whom I spoke in preparing this report, including the following: Joan Acker, Danielle Bazin, Christopher Boorse, Gloria Bowles, Clair Brown, Cristina Bruschini, Constance Buchanan, Constance Carroll, David Cayer, Mariam Chamberlain, Barbara Christian, Arlene Kaplan Daniels, Arlyn Diamond, Bonnie Thornton Dill, Myra Dinnerstein, Betty Parsons Dooley, Estelle Freedman, Mary D. Gordon, Patricia Albjerg Graham, Barbara Haber, Nancy J. Hafkin, Dorothy Helly, Nancy Henley, Arlie Russell Hochschild,

Florence Howe, China Jessup, Robin Lakoff, Susan Lees, Laura Lein, Marjorie Lightman, Margaret Lycette, Ruth B. Mandel, Elaine Marks, Peggy McIntosh, Jean Baker Miller, Nancy K. Miller, Marysa Navarro, Isabel Nieves, Judith Papachristou, Mary Parlee, Diana Pearce, Joseph Pleck, Sarah Rix, Karen Rowe, George Rupp, Joan Wallach Scott, Myra Strober, Gaye Tuchman, Margaret B. Wilkerson, Carolyn G. Wilson, and Marilyn B. Young.

The staff of the Foundation's Education and Culture program and of its Office of Reports were helpful. I am especially grateful to Sheila Biddle and to Gladys Chang Hardy, who was officer in charge of the Education and Culture program while I was a consultant. They were exemplary in the intelligence of their questions and in the consistency of their support.

CATHARINE R. STIMPSON

Introduction

In 1837 Ralph Waldo Emerson, then in his thirties, defined the duties of the American scholar: ". . . to cheer, to raise, and to guide men by showing them facts amidst appearances."[1] Eight years later, his friend Margaret Fuller, then in her thirties, outlined the needs of the American woman, scholar or not:

> What Woman needs is not as a woman to act or to rule, but as a nature to grow, as an intellect to discern, as a soul to live freely and unimpeded, to unfold such powers as were given her . . .[2]

Together, these statements by Emerson and Fuller are prophecies of the goals of women's studies, an intellectual and social movement that has changed what people think and teach about women. Like Emerson, women's studies advocates an active, moral role for scholars; like Fuller, it asserts that women have been less than they could and should be.

A belief in the unity of thought and action is central to women's studies. In this sense, it is quintessentially American. Describing the typical nineteenth-century American, historian Henry Steele Commager spoke of ed-

1

ucation as his religion.[3] What Commager had in mind was the American proclivity to look to education rather than to religion to mold character and to create a new social order. This faith, in large part, explains America's preeminence as an educational innovator. A unique system of education—public, nonsectarian, compulsory, and tax-supported—was established in the United States in the decades before the Civil War. Horace Mann, a contemporary of Emerson and Fuller who is credited with establishing the principle of universal education, believed that "education was . . . a moral renovator" as well as a "great equalizer of human conditions, the balance wheel of the social machinery, and the creator of wealth undreamed of."[4]

Just as Jacksonian reformers created the public school system to instill virtue and sobriety in the citizenry, so colleges structured their studies to build mental discipline and character. The president of Carleton College, J. W. Strong, declared in 1887, "The great aim of every teacher from Socrates to Hopkins has been the building of character."[5]

Since the founding of Harvard College in 1636 until the 1820s, there was little conflict about either the goals or the curricula of American colleges. Colleges were established to train a clergy, to transmit European culture, and to educate an elite. In a culture Puritanism dominated and in a society in which the clergy was the elite, vocational and social goals were one and the same. But as society grew more complex and less homogeneous, consensus about goals and texts broke down.

As early as the 1820s, the traditional curriculum—Greek, Latin, the Bible, and a smattering of science—was challenged by the commercial, industrial, and transportation revolutions. The classics, which had played an important role in the political education of the Founding Fathers and in training the clergy, were not useful to the commercial classes. Throughout the United States, students and public figures demanded a curriculum that would include modern languages—German, French, Spanish, and Italian—and new scientific knowledge. The Governor of New

Hampshire, William Plummer, argued that American education must "pursue a manly and expedient course to fit *men* for the business and duties of this world."[6]

But the sciences remained isolated from collegiate education for the most part until the 1870s. Significantly, by resisting curricular change, higher education in America entered a period of sterility, declining enrollments, and loss of influence on the American scene.[7]

It is appropriate to view women's studies within this framework of a tradition of curricular reform. However, women's studies is itself a response to complex historical circumstances. Catalysts for the growth of women's studies include the political dissent of the 1960s; demographic and educational changes; and the rise of the women's movement, itself inseparable from the long history of women's education.

The Development of
Women's Studies

Women's studies began as a systematic enterprise in American colleges and universities in 1969–1970. At least seventeen courses about women had appeared by that academic year, with the majority in coeducational institutions big enough to afford and flexible enough to permit innovation. A young woman administrator at Cornell University published the outlines prepared for these courses in a single volume—*Female Studies No. 1: A Collection of College Syllabi and Reading Lists*.[8] Ultimately, the *Female Studies* series consisted of ten volumes. By December 1970 more than 100 women's studies courses had been created; by December 1971 there were more than 600. In 1973 there were more than 2,000 courses and 80 women's studies programs on American campuses. Florence Howe, a founder and close observer of this movement, has estimated that at least 20,000 courses and 350 programs existed in 1980.[9] In 1982 another survey reported 30,000 courses.[10]

Together with the women's movement, women's studies has had a profound impact on educational institutions of every kind, altering not only curriculum but also enrollment. Women's studies had some of its deepest origins in history, sociology, and literature, but soon influenced psychology, anthropology, education, political science, and law—as well as the curriculum in secondary and non-credit community schools.[11] Even vocational courses such as woodworking and auto mechanics, which women began to attend in significant numbers for the first time, became infused with a concern for women.

Such impressive curricular growth, aimed at developing women's full capacity, is one of the strongest efforts on behalf of women in the last fifteen years. It was supported by a proliferation of scholarly activity—research, writing, and publishing. Feminist presses and over a dozen journals were established. The body of literature generated was sufficiently large to necessitate two bibliographies of bibliographies.[12] Howe noted that in the first few years there was no distinction between researchers and teachers because teachers were doing their own primary research. "Today," she states, "it's a full-time activity just to read other people's research."[13]

While academics were dealing with women as subjects worthy of study and inquiry, a variety of new organizations began to compel universities to treat women students, faculty, and administrators equitably. In the late 1960s the first of some eighty commissions, caucuses, and committees for and about women in professional associations was formed.[14] The Women's Caucus for Political Science was founded in 1968, followed by the Coordinating Committee for Women in the Historical Profession in 1969, the Society for Women in Philosophy in 1970, and the Committee on Women in Physics in 1971, to mention only a few. In 1970 the American Association of University Professors reactivated Committee W on the Status of Women in the Academic Profession. That same year, the Women's Equity Action League filed the first of hundreds of formal complaints against sex discrimination in universities receiving federal funds.

This explosion of activity did not erupt miraculously. Rather, it required years, even centuries, of agitation on behalf of women's education. Antecedents go back as far

5

as Christine de Pisan (1364–1430?), who defended women's right and ability to be literate, learned, and cultured. Pisan's participation in the lengthy debate about women, the rancorous *querelle des femmes,* anticipated the struggle American women waged for access to education and to the professions in the nineteenth century. By the late nineteenth century that battle, in principle, was won. It would take almost another century for women to gain full acceptance in institutions of higher learning. The struggle for equality within the professions has yet to be won.

The 1920s were a benchmark for women in higher education as they gained "their highest proportion of the undergraduate population, of doctoral recipients . . . of faculty members . . . and constituted nearly 45 percent of the professional [academic] work force."[15] However, these achievements were transitory. Although the proportion of women faculty rose from 19.6 percent to 32.5 percent between 1890 and 1930, it fell to 26.5 percent in 1940 and continued to decline to 22 percent by 1960 where it remained until 1963–1964.[16] Significantly, the number of books about women also declined by the mid-1920s, only to increase again in the mid-1960s.[17]

Before 1920 over half of American college-educated women remained single in order to pursue their professional goals. In the decades between 1920 and 1960, a greater proportion of college-educated women married earlier, had children, and pursued strictly personal goals.[18] With such a decline in career women, it is not surprising that the debate about women's educational needs was renewed in these decades. What kind of education should women receive? When many of America's first women's colleges were founded after the Civil War, the answer was clear: the same as that offered by the most rigorous of men's colleges. Thus, ironically, Bryn Mawr, Mt. Holyoke, Vassar, and Smith adopted a classical curriculum, which included Latin, science, and mathematics, just as it was being phased out at Harvard with the introduction of the elective system.

6

As early as the mid-1920s, some women's colleges were retreating from their original mission. Smith and Vassar instituted courses more "compatible" with women's roles—hygiene, home economics, and the aesthetics of the home. In 1947 Lynn White, president of Mills College, led a movement to create a distinctively feminine curriculum. Arguing that women's colleges should emphasize rather than obliterate differences between men and women, White proposed that women take courses suited to their aptitude. "Women love beauty as much as men do," he asserted, "but they want a beauty connected with the process of living." Women's instincts were "practical and earthy. . . ."[19]

Despite the many setbacks for women in higher education between 1930 and 1960, important efforts were launched or continued in these decades to link education to professional or public achievement. Frequently, they involved an expansion of knowledge about women. In the 1930s, historian Mary Beard tried in vain to establish the World Center for Women's Archives. Using as her slogan the quotation "No documents, no history" from French historian Fustel de Coulanges, Beard started to collect material to provide the basis for a written history. Though Beard's efforts were thwarted by a lack of funds and of an institutional base, three women's history archives were founded in the 1940s—the Sophia Smith Collection at Smith College, the Arthur and Elizabeth Schlesinger Library on the History of Women in America (originally called the Women's Archives) at Radcliffe College, and the National Archives for Black Women's History at the National Council for Negro Women.[20]

For others, a commitment to women's education and careers in academe necessitated the scientific study of sexual difference. Such was the case for many of our foremost women social scientists. The work of Margaret Mead—*Coming of Age in Samoa* (1928) and *Sex and Temperament* (1935)—examined the impact of culture in determining masculine and feminine characteristics. Human nature, she concluded, was "almost unbelievably malleable," based primarily on "differences in conditioning, especially during early childhood."[21] Mead's conclusions and those of the distinguished female social scientists who preceded her— Helen Thompson, Leta Hollingworth, Jessie Taft, Elsie Clews Parsons, and Mary Roberts Coolidge—repudiated the prevailing "scientific" theories of sexual difference. These social scientists, of whom Mead was the most well-known, generated a feminist attack on Victorian theories of female intellectual inferiority and the biologically determined basis of sexual differences. They were joined by Clelia Mosher, doctor for women students at Stanford University, who conducted a pioneering study of female sexuality. In her hygiene course at Stanford, Mosher talked about "the history of women in the world . . . biographies of women . . . writings of psychologists, disputing their claims about women's lack of intellect . . ."[22]

By the 1930s dissident research of this kind had waned. Sociologist Mirra Komarovsky, together with Mead and a few others, continued to investigate sexual difference, but their numbers and influence had declined. The university, which had offered expanded opportunities to white women at the turn of the century, had become a male bastion, more concerned with scientific method than reform. Women graduate students and faculty, their numbers diminished by the Depression, conformed for the most part to the standards and assumptions of the male academy for the next three decades.[23]

Still, a case can be made that the mere presence of women scholars, no matter what their field or point of view, was a powerful argument in favor of professional training for women. A similar case can be made for the women's colleges. Despite the fact that many were conservative supporters of traditional sex roles for women and some had abandoned their goal to educate women as rigorously as men, their mission was the education of women. Equally important, they were the major employer of female academics.

Not surprisingly, the women's colleges played a complex role in the development of women's studies when it was first introduced in the late 1960s and 1970s. The majority opposed women's studies, calling it too aggressively feminist, unnecessary because it already "permeated the curriculum," or a "slightly flaky interdisciplinary backwater." In addition, they argued that it lacked academic standing and would reduce curricular seriousness.[24] Nonetheless, women's colleges produced many of women's studies' most committed supporters and some of its most distinguished practitioners. At one point in the 1970s, a majority of the members of the Commission on the Status of Women of the Modern Language Association were graduates of the same women's college.

One of the most significant efforts to create more educational opportunities for women was launched when the American Council for Education established its Commission on Educational Opportunities for Women in 1953. A landmark conference, held in 1957, explored how institutions could "develop programs that would be responsive to the discontinuities in women's lives."[25] Mary Bunting, president of Radcliffe College, considered inefficient a pattern of education that required full-time study from ages eighteen to twenty-two followed by full-time homemaking from twenty-three to thirty-three. She suggested an eight- to ten-year program of part-time study so that women would be ready for jobs worthy of their talents and education by the time their children were in school. The conference led to the continuing education movement, begun in 1962.

These diverse efforts to enlarge women's educational opportunities and increase knowledge about women's lives, history, and capacities in the four decades after World War I all prepared the ground for the 1960s, which became the critical decade for the growth of women's studies. The political activism and expanding educational opportunities of that decade created an unusually auspicious environment for the women's studies movement.

Women's studies can be seen as one culmination of the protest movements of the 1950s and 1960s—civil rights, the New Left, student activism more generally, black power, and, of course, the women's movement. These origins explain much of the controversy that still surrounds women's studies today. Civil rights leaders pressed for social change by appealing to America's egalitarian principles. The tactics and ideals of Rosa Parks, the Freedom Riders, James Meredith, and Martin Luther King influenced the course, oratory—even the songs—of other protest movements.

For the second time in American history, first in the 1830s and now in the 1960s, "the struggle for racial equality became midwife to the feminist movement."[26] A small core of women activists, armed with the ideology of equality and inspired by the battle against racial injustice, became aware of their unequal treatment as a result of their participation in the civil rights movement. Equally important, the civil rights and black movements gave women experience in organizing and teaching. Florence Howe, for example, adapted techniques she had learned teaching classes in Mississippi for poor black high school students to her women's writing courses at Goucher College.[27]

The New Left, like the civil rights movement, also created a climate of dissent. The New Left had a vision of an egalitarian society—free from poverty, war, racism, and, above all, middle-class hypocrisy. Although more male-dominated than the civil rights movement, the New Left helped raise a substantial following for the women's movement. Some of the first feminist manifestos came from female members of Students for a Democratic Society who argued that they must first fight for their own liberation in order to be effective in a larger revolutionary struggle. Women SDS members set up one of the first women's studies courses at the New Orleans Free School in 1966. (The Free University of Seattle, founded by students at the University of Washington, had already included a women's history course in 1965.) Finally, consciousness-raising, one of

10

the feminist movement's most effective tools for expanding its constituency, had been used by the New Left as an organizing tool.

If the civil rights movement and the New Left provided leadership, a constituency, an ideology, and tactics for the women's movement, student activism and the black power movement created a climate that made it easier to challenge the curriculum taught in colleges and universities throughout the country. Decrying the relevance of what they were taught and demanding participation in university decision making, student activists succeeded in changing or eliminating requirements and adding new courses that explored non-Western cultures. Where blacks had charged ethnocentrism, women were able to attack androcentrism. Blacks insisted on courses that looked at the Afro-American experience; women demanded courses on the female experience.

Black studies and the larger black power movement that helped create black studies made several significant contributions to the theory and practice of women's studies, providing an intellectual agenda for women's studies in its initial phases. The black power movement believed that a revolution by the oppressed must be preceded by a transformation of consciousness in order to succeed. The battle for self-esteem proceeded on two fronts—on the popular level through slogans like "black is beautiful" and in institutions of higher learning through the black studies movement. Black studies, like women's studies after it, sought, first, to reclaim the past and, second, to analyze the causes of oppression.

The Women's Movement

The 1960s revealed deep shifts in the roles and aspirations of women. Historian Alice Kessler-Harris calls the 1950s the decade of the rise of the two-income family.[28] Before World War II, female employment had been limited to young single women and needy married women who were

11

often black; by the 1960s women of all classes and races had entered the public labor force. (By 1975 almost 50 percent of all women worked for wages, with 70 percent of that group at full-time jobs.)[29] Accompanying these major transformations in women's employment patterns were declining birth rates; changing sexual mores, resulting in more flexible family arrangements and alternatives to family life; and a growing demand for equality and personal autonomy.

These changes led to the women's movement—revitalizing feminism as a political force in the United States. In turn, feminism brought women to the fore as a subject of public discussion, debate, and policy, as well as a legitimate focus for scholarly inquiry. Internally, the movement was a "*teaching* movement,"[30] using an oral tradition—conversation and consciousness-raising groups—and the written word—newspapers, poems, or books—to reveal the world and women in a new light.

Feminism inevitably shaped women's studies. Feminist theoreticians outside the university enriched women's studies by the power of their insights. They provided new theories, ideas, and information to be tested in research, refined, and taught. Virginia Woolf, who so brilliantly explained women's cultural marginality, has been central to women's studies. Betty Friedan's *The Feminine Mystique* (1963) and Kate Millett's *Sexual Politics* (1970) ". . . unveiled the ideological nature of the 'values,' 'norms,' and 'beliefs' concerning women's roles and the relations between the sexes . . .";[31] Susan Griffin ("Rape: The All American Crime," 1971) and Susan Brownmiller (*Against Our Will: Men, Women, and Rape*, 1975) wrote of rape, not as a crime of passion that women might provoke, but as a crime of male violence, perpetuating domination over women.

For some, women's studies was feminism's academic "arm." As such, women's studies had three major tasks: teaching the subject of women properly; ending sex discrimination in education on all levels, from pre-kindergarten to postdoctoral study; and integrating feminist activism with feminist thought. Faculty and feminists would nourish each other: Feminists offered scholars links to a broader community of women and an agenda for research, while scholars provided activists a theoretical framework and data to form the basis for social policy and progress. Thus, the scholars had the opportunity to strengthen "the scope of the movement feeding into action against patriarchy."[32] Many women's studies programs (such as that at Sacramento State College in 1971) struggled to hire local feminists to fill teaching roles.

To be sure, feminism posed a moral challenge to scholarship; it asked that research work *for* women. In a widely cited essay published in 1975, psychologist Mary B. Parlee distinguished three types of scholarship about women: "psychology *of* women," often-flawed studies about women; "psychology *against* women," the use of ostensibly objective science to ratify demeaning assumptions about women; and finally, the preferable "psychology *for* women," new or reinterpreted data that exposed misconceptions about women and gender.[33] Researchers in other disciplines were testing similar categories.

These goals led critics to believe that women's studies was nothing but warrior feminism unleashed, hostile to rational thought, common sense, and humane custom, and, as such, illegitimate. Unfortunately, this perception was widespread both on campus and off. Frequently, the links to feminism made women's studies hard to teach. A teacher in the South wryly reported that her female students were:

> ... deeply suspicious of feminism, which appears to be linked in their minds with lesbianism and the devil in a conspiracy to effect passage of the Equal Rights Amendment, which they have been told will lead to chaos.[34]

Such reductionist thinking ignored not only the varieties of feminism, but also the integrity of individual scholars who did not tailor their conclusions to fit their ideologies. For many scholars, female and male, feminism

13

offered political and social values, a normative program. However, women's studies practitioners have been able to reconcile that program with high standards of scholarly research. For example, sociologist Rosabeth Moss Kanter worked hard to avoid the "reductionist thrust [that she perceived] in the intellectual wing of the movement."[35] She embarked on her award-winning book, *Men and Women of the Corporation* (1977), to test a theory she had about the effects of organizational structure on individual consciousness and behavior. In her research, she examined the conditions of work in large organizations, including opportunities for advancement and their influence on how employees behave and direct their lives. She included in her analysis the effects on women of dead-end jobs.

A feminist perspective informs the work of women's studies practitioners, raising questions and concerns that others have ignored. The simplest of these is the question "Where are the women?" Yet posing this question has resulted in an excavation of the history of half the human race. Like the black movement that preceded it, the women's movement placed great importance on uncovering its past. At first, scholars wanted to bring attention to once-prominent women who had been forgotten by history—the so-called women worthies. The motivation for this "compensatory history" was often exhortatory—to find role models, to raise women's consciousness, and to create a positive self-image.

Others, such as the group of women who constituted themselves as "Women on Words and Images" in Princeton, N.J., in 1969, analyzed patterns of sex discrimination in our culture. They studied the presentation of men and women, boys and girls, in over 130 elementary school readers. Their report, *Dick and Jane as Victims*, was one of the "most important scholarly instrument[s] for galvanizing feminist researchers to study and evaluate the entire curriculum with regard to its treatment of women—when they were present at all."[36]

As the field became more sophisticated, scholars and researchers focused on large theoretical concerns such as "Why is occupational segregation so common in Western industrial countries?" The question is a central issue in women's studies because it seeks an explanation for women's unequal status in the contemporary world, and because that unequal status hurts women and children.

While women's studies resurrected women as a proper category for inquiry and analysis, the history of feminism itself gave women's studies impressive historical characters to rediscover—powerful women like Mary Wollstonecraft, the Grimké sisters, Sojourner Truth, Crystal Eastman, Ida B. Wells, and Charlotte Perkins Gilman. The fluctuating reputation of Charlotte Perkins Gilman illustrates not only the fickleness of the American public, but also some of the forces at work in the creation of historical memory. In *Women and Economics* (1898), Gilman argued for the primacy of economic independence for women if they are to achieve equality with men. Though the book was an immediate success—*The Nation* reviewed it as "the most significant utterance on the subject since [John Stuart] Mill's 'Subjugation of Women,' " and it sold very well[37]—Gilman and her work were forgotten until historian Carl Degler published a new edition of *Women and Economics* in 1966. Today Gilman is one of the most influential feminist theoreticians and her writings are required reading in many women's studies courses. Degler suggests that the eclipse and revival of Gilman's reputation was inextricably linked to the fall and subsequent rise of the women's movement.[38]

Others outside women's studies and without public connections to feminism also contributed insights about women's lives. In 1970 a study by economist Ester Boserup, *Women's Role in Economic Development,* exposed how cruelly modernization was changing the sexual division of labor in developing societies. In 1978 Diana Pearce introduced the concept "the feminization of poverty." Her concern arose less from women's studies per se than from her social work education, social concerns, and keen sensitivity to discrimination.[39]

Higher Education in the 1960s

Political activism on campus and curriculum reform were only the most obvious manifestations of the revolution in American higher education in the 1960s. Much more far-reaching were the structural and demographic changes that took place. For the first time in American history, colleges and universities were transformed from elite enclaves into institutions of mass education. The number of students enrolled in college in the decade 1955–1965—3 million—was larger than the *total* number of students enrolled during the previous three centuries in higher education. The 1960s were expansive years in the history of American higher education. Fueled by the postwar baby boom and unprecedented federal and state funding, institutions grew rapidly—in students, faculty, and number.

In such an ebullient climate, higher education had the will and resources to support change and respond to women's educational needs. Curricular change could be achieved relatively painlessly since individual faculty generally had flexibility within departmental guidelines. The multiplicity of purposes of higher education also facilitated the growth of women's studies. Our system of higher education had emerged from the reforms of the 1890s with three conflicting goals and three competing traditions: vocational education, the transmission of liberal culture, and the development of expertise through research and graduate education. By the 1960s the university had also become an instrument for social change dedicated to providing access and social justice. Women's studies could appeal to any or all of these goals.

Moreover, despite the traditionally conservative nature of scholarship, in the 1960s the academy was more open to innovation. The highly influential *The Structure of Scientific Revolutions* (1962) by Thomas Kuhn did much to

16

strengthen skepticism over tradition by showing that even the allegedly "objective" sciences are not value-free. Rather, paradigms—basic assumptions about how the world works—shape them. Individual disciplines were also undergoing reevaluation. The new social history, for example E. P. Thompson's *The Making of the English Working Class* (1963), was examining the experience of ordinary people, the conditions of daily work, and the fluctuations of the life cycle. It became a logical ally of women's studies. A group exploring the origins of women's history stated:

> Feminism has provided an agenda for research, while social history brings methods and sources to the enterprise; both have been necessary and neither has been sufficient.[40]

In this hospitable atmosphere, increasing numbers of people were sufficiently interested in or tolerant of women's studies to provide either active support or a sympathetic reception. Some of the most important of these people were men—men responsive to women's issues, to educational reform, or to both. Again and again, a male dean, vice president, department chairperson, or foundation officer gave a women's studies project essential moral and material aid. Obviously, there were more female supporters than male. Even though the proportion of women in higher education had shrunk by 1960, enough remained to make women's studies possible. Of course, the greater the number of women in a discipline, the more likely was women's studies to grow in that discipline.

17

Institutionalizing
a Field of Study

Though women's studies has greatly altered the world of scholarship, its impact on the university as a whole has been less pervasive—once again showing that ideas are more responsive to change than are institutions. Scholars outside women's studies are far more likely to include an article on the history of child care in their research than to support a child-care center at their colleges. A professional association would rather endorse women's studies than affirmative action or paid parental leave.

The development of women's studies from a dissident movement into a respectable field of study—replete with libraries, archives, presses, journals, research institutes, programs, and courses—is a case study in legitimation. Its evolution can only be suggested here. As noted, women's studies received a vital impetus from the social and political activism of the 1960s and from the war of ideas waged by feminist theoreticians. Necessity, sociological insight, and ideology combined to persuade some feminists of the need to build women's studies outside traditional academic structures. Women faculty and graduate students, who were in a distinct minority in the 1960s but whose numbers were increasing, brought these ideas inside the university.

There, other women were independently developing them. Gerda Lerner, then teaching at the New School for Social Research, and the late Annette Baxter of Barnard College taught the first women's history courses in the early 1960s.

Women's studies pioneers varied by age, politics, discipline, and academic status when they entered the field; however, they all shared a public commitment to women's issues and research before women's studies formally cohered as a field in the late 1960s. Among the earliest and most significant works are sociologists Jessie Bernard's *Academic Women* (1964) and Alice Rossi's "Equality between the Sexes: An Immodest Proposal" (1964), and historians Gerda Lerner's *The Grimké Sisters* (1967) and Anne Firor Scott's *The Southern Lady* (1970). Scott and Lerner, who both have served as president of the Organization of American Historians, started to write women's history as graduate students. After working in the national headquarters of the League of Women Voters in Washington, D.C., from 1944–1947, Scott entered graduate school at Harvard, only to find no recognition of the role of women in politics. To redress the balance, Scott wrote an early seminar paper on the importance of women's organizations in the community. Her subject was so poorly received that she devoted only a page and a half of her doctoral dissertation on southern progressives in Congress to women. Scott argues today that that page and a half was arguably the only original part of her thesis. She returned to the subject of women for a faculty seminar at Chapel Hill in 1958 and completed her book twelve years later.[41]

Gerda Lerner, born in 1920 in Austria, is a contemporary of Scott's. Like many women of that generation, Lerner returned to school after raising a family. As a graduate student at Columbia University from 1963 to 1966, she was permitted to write a dissertation on the Grimké sisters. Rossi completed her doctoral training in sociology at Columbia University in 1957. She wrote her essay while she was a research associate, a position she held at a number of institutions until she got her first tenure-track academic appointment in 1969. Rossi's correspondence with two friends about problems confronting women sociologists led to the formation of a women's caucus at the American Sociological Association in 1969 and to an important survey of female employment in sociology graduate programs. Jessie Bernard, on the other hand, was a senior scholar when she wrote *Academic Women*. Though Bernard did not consider herself to be a militant feminist at the time she wrote her book, she wrote "to vindicate the rights of women."[42]

Scott, Lerner, Rossi, and Bernard were all isolated scholars responding to an incipient feminism. By the next generation, connections were forged across generations, between students and faculty, and between scholarship and politics. This emerges clearly in the career of Sara Evans, a historian on the faculty at the University of Minnesota who wrote her dissertation on the relation between women's liberation, the civil rights movement, and the New Left, later published as *Personal Politics* (1979). Evans, born in 1943, was an undergraduate at Duke University, where she met Anne Scott. In 1967, Evans joined a women's liberation group in Chicago and became ". . . a quiet but passionate participant in what we all believed was a historic undertaking: the creation of a new, radical feminist movement."[43] She entered graduate school in 1969, determined to study women's history as Scott had done.

As courses proliferated, women's studies practitioners tried to change the teaching process and its hierarchy of authority. An anti-authoritarian bias was built into the curriculum and teaching methods used in women's studies courses. Individual teachers had different visions of an egalitarian classroom, to be sure, but their teaching was aimed at empowering previously powerless "inferior" groups. The actual creation of such classrooms could be a delicate and demanding task. For such a classroom to work, male students often had to abandon automatic presumptions of authority while female students had to acquire a sense of personal authority. In 1982, a student added this note to her final exam on women writers:

> I have even surprised my fiancé when I asserted myself on certain issues. I surprised him to the point where he said, "What, is the women's lib getting to you, you never felt this way before." But I realized I had always felt this way before. I just never said it outright.[44]

The proliferation of courses led to the creation of coherent women's studies programs. Between 1970 and 1975, 150 such programs were established; by 1980 the number had reached 300.[45] In addition to developing an intellectual focus, these programs began to grant credentials such as a certificate, a major, or a minor; to sponsor lectures, seminars, and meetings; to offer small research stipends; and to provide counseling. Women's studies programs also came to serve as a general resource on women's scholarship and teaching for the entire campus. They now exist on at least 450 campuses as diverse as the University of Santa Clara, a Jesuit institution in California; Northern Illinois University, a state school in the Midwest; Barnard College, a private women's college in New York; and Bennett College, a black college in North Carolina. In the Ivy League, only Harvard still lacks a program. Paradoxically, some evidence suggests that women's studies is more likely to exist at institutions with few women on the faculty (0 to 19 percent) than at those with many.[46] It is as though, outnumbered, women can find a source of group security and activity in women's studies.

Academic programs conferred greater respectability on women's studies as a field than isolated courses had, but it remained for those who did research—through the power of their ideas and the excellence of their scholarship—to confer legitimacy on the field. Scholarship and research were encouraged through the usual protocol of academic conferences and symposia as well as in response to the need of the new courses and programs for anthologies and textbooks. New institutions made the new scholarship about women accessible to both the scholarly community and beyond. Journals and presses were created. KNOW, the first publisher of *Female Studies,* was founded in Pittsburgh in 1969. Florence Howe and Paul Lauter were instrumental in creating Feminist Press in 1970. In 1972 three interdisciplinary journals—*Women's Studies, Feminist Studies,* and *Women's Studies Newsletter*—were established. *Signs* appeared in 1975.

Of course, some institutions necessary for the growth of women's studies were in place long before the women's studies movement. For example, the Schlesinger Library at Radcliffe College was founded in 1943. Despite scant regard for women's history among historians and the public at large, the Schlesinger Library kept collecting valuable materials that in the 1970s would enable it to strengthen scholarship in women's history. The Schlesinger Library and the Sophia Smith Collection at Smith College have radically changed with the rise of the women's movement and the growth of women's studies. Patricia King, director of the Schlesinger Library, first worked there as a graduate student in the early 1960s. "In those days," she recalls, "if anyone walked through the door we had a celebration." Such joyous occasions had jumped from 247 in 1970 to over 4,000 in 1980. Success breeds competition, and today most major research libraries are striving to build up their women's history collections.[47]

The general availability of public and private financial support was another important reason why women's studies took off so vigorously. Large-scale faculty and curriculum growth would not have been possible without support from several key foundations. Grants and fellowships nurtured individual scholars and helped confer credibility on the new field. Among the private foundations that played a central role were the Ford Foundation, Carnegie Corporation, the Rockefeller Foundation, the Rockefeller Brothers Fund, the Andrew W. Mellon Foundation, the Helena Rubinstein Foundation, the Russell Sage Foundation, the Exxon Education Foundation, the Eli P. Lilly Foundation, and the Revson Foundation. Public agencies included the National Endowment for the Humanities and its state councils, the Fund for the Improvement of Post-Secondary Education, the National Institute of Education, and the office of the Women's Education Equity Act.

Of these, the Ford Foundation was clearly the leader. As early as 1959, it provided funding for a Rutgers University study of women in mathematics and a grant to the Radcliffe Institute for part-time scholarships and career guidance. Between 1972 and 1975, the Foundation gave out 130 postdoctoral fellowships and dissertation awards in women's studies. Fifty percent of the senior people it supported became prominent in women's studies, as did at least one-third of the people in the dissertation program. Between 1964 and 1979, Ford gave a total of $30 million to advocacy, research, and curriculum projects in women's studies.[48]

As of 1983, nationwide, about ten fellowship programs were in existence for either woman scholars or scholarship about women. In addition, faculty seminars at some institutions offer the equivalent of mini-fellowships. Unfortunately, a majority of these programs depend on "soft" money. Their lack of permanent funding increases the unpredictability of the development of women's studies and decreases the field's ability to secure support for important constituencies. Among those most vulnerable are graduate students, to whom a grant as small as $1,000 can make a difference,[49] postdoctoral scholars in a bleak job market, and intellectual pioneers who want to integrate women's studies with such fields as peace studies, poverty studies, or black studies and, thus, do not easily fit within disciplinary boundaries.

The Women's Research Centers

During the 1970s previously isolated courses, programs, and archives coalesced into a national network of institutions. One of the most crucial developments was the emergence of a national system of research centers, each of which assumed specific regional tasks. The Radcliffe Institute, established in 1960 as a center of independent scholarship by women, was the first. By the early 1980s, as many as fifty regional centers had been created. Unlike the Radcliffe Institute (now called the Mary Ingraham Bunting Institute), these centers were concerned not simply with scholarship *by* women, but also *about* them. The Ford Foundation provided support close to $3 million to help such centers.

Today those research centers rely on a variety of funding sources: home institutions, government, corporations, private donors, foundations, publishing sales, and consultancies. A bequest to the Center for the Study of Women in Society at the University of Oregon—though highly unusual—dramatizes the importance of a tradition of women's mutual support. Established by the University of Oregon faculty in the early 1970s, the center received only minimal financial support until it came to the notice of William Harris. In fulfillment of the wishes of his late wife Jane Grant, feminist, journalist, and a founder of *The New Yorker,* Harris left his estate to the university to support women's activities. In 1983 the center began to receive the income from the $3.5 million bequest, which it will spend on research.[50]

The centers have diverse institutional arrangements.[51] Some, like the Institute for Research in History, the Equity Policy Center, the International Center for Research in Women, the Center for Women Policy Studies, and the Program of Policy Research on Women and Families, are independent. Many of these institutions are located in Washington, D.C., because government officials and policy makers are their most important constituency. Others, such as the Office of Women in Higher Education of the American Council on Education and the Project on the Status and Education of Women of the Association of American Colleges, are part of larger, free-standing institutions. Still others, the majority, operate within colleges and universities. They have the advantages of libraries and information services, the cooperation of a local women's studies program, the university's legitimacy, and such direct assistance as staff support, telephones, space, and a little program money. However, when funding is cut, the budgets of women's studies centers are often among the first to be reduced. Even when universities are financially secure, their support for women's research centers can be grudging and sparse.

Although the women's research centers and programs address a wide range of issues, the dominant issue on the research agenda is the nexus of women, work, and family. For example, a 1982 survey of twenty-seven centers found fifty-seven different research projects exploring questions on women and the family.[52] The centers also initiate and administer numerous projects. In 1982 the Southwest Institute for Research on Women started a three-year teacher-training program to increase nonsexist, multicultural curricula in rural high schools in the Southwest; a three-week institute to introduce women's history to high school teachers; a research conference on sex differences in language; and a conference for humanists and public policy people on mid-life crisis.[53]

Finally, many centers, such as Feminist Press and Women's Interart Center, offer other services in addition to research, training, and curriculum development. Some, such as the Center for the Study, Education, and Advancement of Women at the University of California (Berkeley), the Center for Women Policy Studies, Higher Education Resources Services, and the Women's Research and Education Institute, work for institutional change, counsel women, or provide a forum for feminist concerns outside large urban areas. The Michigan Center for Continuing Education for Women, which opened in 1964, works in a variety of areas. It does research on education, work, and the life cycle; advises women reentering the work force and serves as their university advocate; maintains data and a library; and sponsors conferences.

The centers have become a national resource. More flexible than academic departments, they may house free-lance scholars or fellowship programs, as well as regular faculty members. The centers experiment with new ideas, collaborate on research, and run pilot programs that serve as models to be adopted elsewhere. They also train administrators. At the least, they provide a base for women and their concerns within institutions that might otherwise prefer to ignore them. Within their sphere, the centers accomplish what women's colleges once did within higher education as a whole.

The centers have been creative with their resources, but they now confront a painful dilemma. Because it takes between six and eight years of general support for a center to become self-sufficient, many of them have not had time to achieve financial security. The climate of funding for women and research on women, especially if it is explicitly feminist, has chilled. The Center for the American Woman and Politics at Rutgers University received its first grant from Ford in 1971, but could not stop worrying "every day [about] the question of survival without Ford support until 1977."[54] The center needed time to train a staff, establish a record, use outside money as leverage for university support, and gain credibility. In 1982 it had an average annual budget of $350,000, a staff of about ten, work-study helpers and interns, and a unique reputation for research about women's political participation. The Wellesley Center, founded in 1974 with a Carnegie Corporation grant, is now among the most productive of the centers. In 1982 its staff consisted of forty-four men and women. In 1980–81 its income was $1,670,745.[55] Yet even the Wellesley Center could use more program money. The centers must, in fact, compete with each other for increasingly limited funding.

The diverse individuals, activities, and institutions concerned with women's studies are tied together by two umbrella organizations—the National Council for Research on Women, founded in 1982, and the National Women's Studies Association, founded in 1977. The National Council for

26

Research on Women, located in New York, coordinates the activities of the research centers. It encourages collaborative inquiry, keeps a data bank on women's research, distributes publications, and publicizes the centers.

The goals of the National Women's Studies Association are more far-reaching—nothing short of a complete transformation of consciousness and institutions. In the preamble to its constitution, NWSA states its fundamentally revolutionary position:

> Women's studies owes its existence to the movement for the liberation of women; the women's liberation movement exists because women are oppressed. Women's studies, diverse as its components are, has at its best shared a vision of a world free not only from sexism but also from racism, class bias, ageism, heterosexual bias—from all the ideologies and institutions that have consciously or unconsciously oppressed and exploited some for the advantage of others.

The organization that emerged reflects its ambitious aims. NWSA brings together women's studies practitioners and supporters from every setting—pre-kindergarten programs to research institutes. It has lively annual conferences such as the one in 1980 that confronted the issues of racism and anti-Semitism. Regrettably, its governing structure—a complex of councils, committees, and caucuses—has been unwieldy, and its ambitions have exceeded its financial resources. In 1982, debts threatened NWSA with collapse, but it was able to restructure its administration and balance its budget.[56] In 1983 NWSA had over 2,000 members, 15 percent more than in 1982 and 40 percent more than in 1981. Today its future seems more secure.

Women's studies today reflects the strengths and weaknesses of its ambitious yet diverse origins. In 1971 literary critic Elaine Showalter wrote:

> Women's studies did not spring full-blown from the head of the women's liberation movement; nor was it the daughter of the civil rights movement, or the youth culture, or the free university movement, although all of these clearly

played a part in its development. When we realize that there were almost as many circumstances giving rise to the course as there were courses, we may understand why there is no unifying ideology for women's studies.[57]

The multiplicity of causes for women's studies led to a profusion of theory and practice. The virtues of this proliferation were obvious: energy, a cross-fertilization of ideas, and the opportunity for individuals and local programs to work out their own definition of women's studies. However, the lack of a unifying ideology also led to controversy, occasionally severe enough to destroy a program. Major conflicts arose over questions of institutional affiliation, organizational structure, and nomenclature. In the final analysis, these disputes were ideological, reflecting tensions between the academic and political goals of women's studies.

The question of university affiliation provoked strong arguments. Would a women's studies program survive within a college or university? Could it work authentically—i.e., preserve the goals of the women's studies movement or would it be co-opted into the establishment, an establishment that had once excluded women? To put the question another way, are radical feminist goals compatible with the university system and structure? Powerful voices argued against university affiliation. At an important women's studies conference held at the University of Pennsylvania in 1974, Adrienne Rich called for a "university-without-walls" to integrate culture and politics:

> Programs in the universities, yes; but more significantly, . . . [the] university-without-walls which has taken root across the country and in many other parts of the world during the last few years. We are seeing the new knowledge already being disseminated and turned into action: Self-help clinics, arts centers, rape crisis centers, abortion centers, bookstores. . . .[58]

Unfortunately, autonomous women's studies programs rarely succeed unless they offer such practical services as legal help. A case in point is Sagaris, an independent school for feminist theory and women's studies, organized as a collective by a group of women in 1974. The brochure for its first two sessions, which took place in Vermont in 1975, announced:

> There are now many feminist programs within degree-granting colleges. Sagaris, because of its independence and excellent faculty, will reach beyond the scope of what can be accomplished within more traditional institutions.

In 1976 Sagaris reorganized as "an independent, multi-racial institute for the study of feminist politics" and publicized classes for 1977. But Sagaris died before the term began—beset by financial and administrative difficulties and by quarrels over feminist politics so passionate that a group of students and faculty walked out of the second of the two 1975 sessions to set up alternative meetings.

Disagreement over governance has been at once organizational and political. How should a program be run? Who should control it—students, faculty, or both? Should it include community women and activists to maintain its ties to the outside world? How can a program be anti-hierarchical, anti-authoritarian, and collectivist and still function? The avowed political goals of some advocates of women's studies raise serious policy issues with no easy solutions. For example, what is the responsibility of women's studies to women, feminism, and other movements for social change? Should a program accept foundation money or would this demonstrate too great a readiness to compromise with society?

Controversy over the status of women's studies within the university involved intellectual and theoretical issues too. Was women's studies a discipline like history or English, requiring its own department—or an area of inquiry in which all the disciplines participated? From the beginning, women's studies challenged the traditional disciplines. Kate Millett's *Sexual Politics* (1970), which she started as a doctoral dissertation in English at Columbia University, was an early model. It both pushed at the boundaries of literary criticism, through interpreting books in fresh ways, and ranged beyond to incorporate law, history, psychology, sociology, and politics. The debate about the status of women's studies as a discipline has persisted in theoretical discussions and in the practical matter of designing a program, curriculum, and students' schedules.

As women's studies grew during the 1970s, political quarrels abated, but they never disappeared. Indeed, controversies increased as women's studies focused on prominent public issues. In the 1980s a correspondent to the newsletter of the Association of Women in Science threatened to resign if AWIS took a stand on nuclear armaments. Nuclear weapons, she said, had nothing to do with the single reason why she joined AWIS, to advance women in science.[59]

Nothing illustrates the way these issues are tied together better than the dispute over naming women's studies. For a name signifies governance, affiliations, politics, and organization. In the early 1970s several candidates were put forward. "Feminist studies" overtly declares its political origins and intentions. "Sex-role [or 'gender'] studies" strives for greater objectivity by suggesting a comparative social scientific methodology to examine patterns of masculinity and femininity and at the same time implies that the difference between men and women is social rather than biological. "Female studies," like "sex-roles studies," is a neutral term, but its scope is limited to one sex, and it seems to be more biologically oriented than "gender studies." Finally, there is "women's studies" itself. (During the 1970s "feminology," "women studies," and "dimorphics" were also suggested.) To a degree, feminist studies and sex-role (or gender) studies can be seen as opposite ends of a spectrum of commitment to feminist theory and practice. More neutral than feminist studies, but more committed to women than sex-role studies, women's studies became the common term.

A number of strategies, many of which had their origins in feminist ideology and the women's movement, were useful in preventing disagreements from dominating women's studies. As part of a general egalitarian commitment, people wanted to discuss disputes openly. The belief that women have a right to self-determination justified a variety of different answers and identities. The feminist emphasis on cooperation, affiliation, and sisterhood manifested itself in the way meetings were conducted, in the generous distribution of reading lists and syllabi, and in the building of networks. In 1971 one national and over fourteen regional conferences were held. Rapidly, women's studies built up an informal cadre of speakers who went from campus to campus as lecturers and consultants. They simultaneously encouraged the autonomy of local programs and a sense of participation in a national movement.

The rapid expansion of women's studies also prevented a destructive, abrasive divisiveness. This growth was clear evidence that women's studies was meeting a real need. The increasing presence of women in higher education, partly because of affirmative action, helped stimulate the growth.[60] In 1965 women earned 10 percent of all doctorates; by 1979 the percentage was nearly 29 percent. By 1977 the proportion of women among faculty members had risen to 31.7 percent. Of course, increased numbers alone do not guarantee women secure positions or prestige,[61] and not all women academics go into women's studies. Nevertheless, the pool of available students, faculty, and administrators widened and deepened.

As women's studies matured in the 1970s, it sustained its moral belief in equity. It continued to support advocacy projects, affirmative action efforts, and such legislative initiatives as Title IX of the Higher Education Amendments (1972), which forbade sex discrimination in educational institutions receiving federal aid. As a field of inquiry, women's studies developed in two ways. On the one hand, it became more heterogeneous. This was the welcome result of growth: more courses, more programs, more specialization within divergent academic disciplines, and more varied perspectives, such as those of women of color. On the other hand, women's studies became more institutionalized. It nurtured an educational identity and ethos. In brief, diversity and stability sought a peaceful coexistence.

Women's Studies:
Issues and Approaches

The experience of many people in women's studies in the late 1960s and the 1970s should be familiar in outline to students of psychological and cognitive change. It began with a sense of rupture and estrangement from accepted knowledge, with the discovery that such knowledge excluded, distorted, or trivialized the self. Dale Spender, editor and writer, says she became "vigilantly suspicious of everything" she knew.[62] This skepticism extended from ordinary clichés—for example, "women's place is in the home"—to sophisticated psychoanalytic theories that viewed woman as castrated man. Skepticism and negation were not ends in themselves; they preceded a joyous rediscovery of women's genuine experience, a re-creation of reality. This revision began by treating woman as a subject "in a material and local world."[63] It proceeded in two stages, an epistemological deconstruction and reconstruction, that were at once individual and collective.

A well-known example of this process of deconstruction and reconstruction is Carol Gilligan's *In A Different Voice* (1982). In this study of women's moral development, Gilligan reexamines the notion—rampant in psychological literature since Freud—that women lack a highly developed sense of morality. Lawrence Kohlberg, her colleague at Harvard, had delineated six stages of moral development in the ascent from childhood to maturity. According to Kohlberg, girls and women reached only the third plateau of moral development, a stage where goodness is equated with helping and pleasing others. Men and even boys, on the other hand, were situated on the fourth, fifth, and sixth rungs, where relationships are subordinated to rules and principles of universal justice. Gilligan points out that Kohlberg constructed his stages by observing a sample of eighty-four boys. By including women and girls in her research, Gilligan discovered that males and females did have different ethical processes and standards, but the female standard was neither simplistic nor inferior.

> When one begins with the study of women and derives developmental constructs from their lives, the outlines of a moral conception different from that described by Freud, Piaget or Kohlberg begin to emerge. . . . In this conception, the moral problem arises from *conflicting* responsibilities rather than from *competing* rights and requires for its resolution a mode of thinking that is cultural and narrative rather than formal and abstract. This conception of morality . . . centers moral development around the understanding of respect and relationships just as the conception of morality as fairness ties moral development to the understanding of rights and rules.[64]

The explosion of knowledge about women has been so rapid that students and researchers who entered the field by the mid-1970s cannot claim to have been pioneers. Because of the impact of women's studies on other fields, newcomers were less estranged from the curriculum, less excited by the prospect of revising it. Simultaneously, the pioneers became less marginal as their early work became accepted, influenced others, and informed new research. Carroll Smith-Rosenberg, a founder of women's history, has said:

> We have so quickly become part of the professional mainstream, leaders in the new social history, that it is easy to forget the spirit of those early years. Nor have younger

scholars just becoming aware of women's history any way of knowing the fervor we brought to our task or with what elation and camaraderie we turned to each other.[65]

Casual observers of women's studies may underestimate how large and refined it has become as an intellectual enterprise. Investigating the subject of women within specific disciplines and across disciplinary boundaries, women's studies has generated several constellations of questions, theories, and facts. The first constellation grew out of the simple but challenging assumption that women as a group are a legitimate subject of scholarly study. Precisely how this would be carried out was problematic. Should women be treated as a class, a caste, or a biological category? No matter which mode of analysis was employed, women's studies quickly documented how much women's experience had differed from that of men. Such adventurous intellects as Gerda Lerner, Juliet Mitchell, and the late Joan Kelly argued that the categories we all use to think about history required a radical revision in order to take women's lives and experience into account. Suppose, historian Joan Kelly suggested in her 1977 essay "Did Women Have a Renaissance?" that women's lives during the Renaissance did not enjoy a rebirth, but rather underwent a contraction. If so, to use the word "Renaissance" would be, at best, an ironic joke.

In codifying women's experience, scholars have developed two different, though not mutually exclusive, methods. Some scholars concentrated on women's *separate* histories, culture, work, and habits, while others were more intent on examining the structure or systemic arrangements in society that shaped men's and women's lives. An influential exposition of the latter method was published in 1975 by Gayle Rubin, then a graduate student in anthropology at the University of Michigan. She argued that just as psychoanalysts have shown us how we organize our unconscious lives, economists our goods and services, anthropologists our kinship systems, so women's studies can illuminate the structures erected to organize our dimorphism—the social architecture of gender, of femininity and masculinity—that we have built on the biological grounds of the sexual division of the species into female and male. Rubin's work reflects what has become a cornerstone of women's studies, the distinction between gender and sex.[66]

Documentation of sexism in women's lives and in their education was another goal of women's studies scholarship. All women's studies scholars agree that relations between men and women involve questions of power. Comparatively, more men have wielded power over women than women over men. Sexism, sex discrimination, and sexual stratification are undeniable realities. According to feminist economist Barbara Bergmann,

> . . . employment discrimination [was] . . . not a personal foible of the individuals who make hiring decisions, but [derived] from a system of social organization in which woman's role is as a servant of men. The existence of this tradition influences the behavior of individuals, men and women, even as they carry on their economic business.[67]

The consensus about women's comparative powerlessness broke apart over the *universality* of their subordination. Some, influenced by Simone de Beauvoir's *The Second Sex,* espoused the view that women have always been subordinate. Others, using theories of Friedrich Engels or Mary Beard, argued that societies did exist, or had once existed, in which women shared a rough parity with men. The latter group raised profound questions about social change and changing gender roles. If women once had equality with men, when and why did it end? How do such large-scale social changes as urbanization or development affect men and women *qua* men and women? Must one sex gain at the expense of the other?

The study of sexism had a profound impact on students. In classes throughout the country, some students, female and male, found reports of discrimination exaggerated, melodramatic, and self-serving; while others saw the world in a new way. Still others became angry and depressed. Teachers throughout the country revised courses to show that an analysis of sexism need not lead to inertia or sorrowful stupor but to strategies for change. At Oregon State University, enrollment declined in the introductory women's studies course until 1978, when it was redesigned "to bring an analytical rigor" to women's issues and to specify the goals of the course "in a positive way."[68] At the University of Colorado/Colorado Springs, a faculty member concluded:

> We know from our classes in Women's Studies the importance of pushing our criticism past itself to the visions that the criticism suggests. Unless we do that, we offer no hope for directing the anger that is often generated by the critical awareness, and we are left with paralyzing fury or hopeless resignation. ("Is this another moan course?" a Women's Studies major asked on the first day of class.)[69]

These strategic shifts in curriculum in the 1970s paralleled changes in women's studies scholarship. Much of the early scholarship, particularly inquiries into the causes of women's oppression, treated women as victims—"sad sacks" of socialization, passive, without any past. During the 1970s, other important studies of women as victims continued to appear, including research on racism, rape, incest, and sexual harassment. However, as women gained a past, traditions, and a history of accomplishments, they began to appear more powerful and vibrant. In keeping with this new image, historians began to treat women as active agents, in charge of their destinies though sometimes subject to the tyranny and folly of others. In the mid-1970s Adrienne Germain urged institutions, organizations, and governments to plan for women's development and economic self-sufficiency, not for welfare services. She asked that programs have their root in a knowledge of the "... *facts* of women's lives, not [in]. . . idealized role and status concepts. Recognize," she said, "women's *strengths*, not simply their 'problems.' "[70]

Through new research and greater awareness, women of color became an important model of strength for many women in the United States. The Center for Research on

Women at Memphis State University has pioneered studies on the intersection of race, class, and gender—a compelling, but still unresolved issue. Collaboration between women's studies and minority studies has been facilitated by conferences such as the one held at the University of Massachusetts at Amherst, "Black Studies/Women's Studies: An Overdue Partnership," in 1983.

No matter which path their research took, women's studies scholars inevitably had to confront the issue of sexual difference. Are men and women different? How? How much is biological? Cultural? Until scholars began to ask these hard questions, sexual difference was viewed either as a joyous fact of life—"*Vive la différence*"—or as part of the order of things, too entrenched to be challenged. Traditional scholarship tended to accept these notions, buttressing bias with psychological measures of masculinity and femininity that equated *masculine* with health and normality, *feminine* with neurosis and abnormality.

Women's studies, on the other hand, began to analyze the psychological, social, and cultural manifestations of difference. Led by historians and anthropologists, scholars conceptualized reality as two separate spheres. Males inhabited a public sphere of productive activity, political power, and cultural authority. This was the domain of the father and of the son. Females lived in a privatized, domestic world of reproductive activity, political marginality, and discontinuous cultural authority. This was the domain of the mother and of the daughter. Each sphere had its own work, although there was some crossing over—for example, women working in offices, essentially part of the male world.

The study of male and female worlds followed many paths that frequently crossed. One path examined women's association with the domestic sphere to explain their subordinate status. A second studied a wide range of women's worlds that varied in scale, scope, and purpose. It looked at purdah, women's political movements, including feminism, women's clubs, lesbian subcultures, schools, and prisons. Scholars found that women's institutions—colleges, convents, and associations—enhanced women's self-esteem and strength. If women had some social space that they controlled, they were empowered—at least partially.[71] Such evidence was invaluable for the supporters of women's colleges who resisted the lemming-like rush to coeducation in the early 1970s.

A third path charted the motives, performance, difficulties, and success of women who entered the male world, especially as wage earners. Films like *Rosie the Riveter* popularized the dignity and deprivations of such a passage, and there have also been scholarly analyses of women in male worlds. Alice Kessler-Harris published an account of wage-earning women in the United States in 1982; Cynthia Fuchs Epstein a sociology of women lawyers in 1981; Judith Stiehm a narrative of women's admission to the Air Force Academy in 1981; Elaine Showalter a study of women novelists who entered the masculinized world of culture in 1977; and Jeane J. Kirkpatrick a picture of women in state legislatures in 1974.[72]

At the same time, women's studies stimulated a new interest in the subject of men. Though women's studies had earlier called the traditional fields of scholarship "men's studies" because they ignored women, the new "men's studies" now examined masculinity as a social construct that took its toll even while granting power and privilege.

Another approach was to study the family, the terrain on which men and women commingle so closely. This path took several directions. One aimed at a precise description of family roles: work (such as housework), power, and identity. In the studies of Nancy Chodorow, among others, the family emerged as the crucible of gender identity.[73] Through historical or anthropological inquiry, others sought alternatives to the nuclear family. A variation on this theme was the effort to ascertain how and when the nuclear family appeared. Others analyzed problems of women in families today. Among these are child abuse and wife-battering, incest, and the double burden of house- and wage-work.

Women's studies has also examined how social policies, based on the assumption that women are primarily wives and mothers, have made women's lives more difficult—both outside and inside the home. Lenore J. Weitzman, a sociologist who had taught one of the earliest women's studies courses, examined the effects of the California no-fault divorce law. She found that, on the average, the husband's standard of living had risen 42 percent one year after a divorce, while the wife's had declined 73 percent. She then stated:

> The time has come for us to recognize that divorced women and their children need greater economic protection—and to fashion remedies to accomplish that goal.[74]

In the mid-1970s the inquiry into sexual differences turned into a debate between "minimalists" and "maximalists." The majority of women's studies scholars hold a minimalist position about sexual difference. They acknowledge difference—both biological and sociological—between men and women, but contend that such differences as work, life spans, moral capacities, speech, and aptitudes have been shaped by historical rather than by cosmic or hormonal forces. Sociologist Cynthia Fuchs Epstein sums up the current minimalist position:

> On the basis of current research, the biological differences between men and women have little or no relevance to their behavior and capacities apart from the sexual and reproductive roles; even the effects of early gender socialization may be reversed by adult experiences. A growing body of knowledge indicates that, under the same conditions, men and women show similar competence, talent, ambition, and desire in activities that range from running races to doing scientific research. That conditions vary so regularly and decisively for men and women has more to do with divisions of power in society than with innate sex difference.[75]

Given different historical circumstances and conditioning, sexual difference could become irrelevant or everyone could become "androgynous."

Maximalists sharply dispute the theory that social conditioning is the basis for gender difference. They argue that deep, transcultural forces cause many sex differences and that the connection between sex, a biological category, and gender, a social one—far from being trivial—is more profound than minimalists believe. Maximalists also contend that these differences, though deep-seated, are no basis for inequality and do not justify women's subservience within the family, community, and state.

The debate between minimalists and maximalists is significant—not only politically, but also intellectually. At the moment, there are at least four different maximalist approaches. The first is associated with the work of Carol Gilligan, and the second with Alice Rossi. Both urge caution in tampering with sex differences. Rossi argues that sex differences are essentially bioevolutionary—that is, the product of biological forces, rooted primarily in the endocrine system and in the need for species survival. She gives salience to the body as a lawgiver of social relations and urges scholars to look at parenting from a perspective that recognizes that women bear and rear children for evolutionary and physiological reasons. An egalitarian approach to parenting is both unrealistic—requiring "compensatory education" for men—and potentially harmful to mothers and children.[76] Gilligan, on the other hand, offers no explanation for gender differences, but argues that female characteristics should be preserved because they are good in and of themselves.

A third position, associated with certain French feminist theoreticians, celebrates female difference. They believe that difference is most profoundly revealed in language. They locate the causes of difference in the structures of the body, of mother-child and father-child relationships, of the unconscious, and of desire. A fourth school, "revisionary maximalism," views difference between men and women as biological, based on women's reproductive capacities. As the importance of that role diminishes in the modern world, however, the reasons for difference, and the difference itself, should fade away. Thus historian Mary Hartman says,

> What was truly remarkable about the "capitalist" era was not the labor, paid or unpaid, that women performed but instead the slow undoing of the links between their biological selves and the roles available for them to play in society. What had happened to men centuries before now happened to women, as the bonds which had always confined women's world within narrower limits than men's were loosened.[77]

The debate between these various points of view will be difficult to resolve. The relation between nature and nurture, biology and culture, is too complex, subtle, and dynamic to admit of any precise and final measurement. Even if one could be derived, it might be an inappropriate guide for policy. Moreover, similarities between men and women are greater than their differences. To emphasize difference over similarity polarizes human nature and reinforces sexual duality as a basis for society.

In addition, emphasis on sexual difference obscures the vital recognition of differences among women. In the United States, women of color demonstrated that ideas about white women do not always apply to them.[78] A serious study of the impact of racial oppression on women's lives could add an international dimension to women's studies, linking it to the study of South Africa, for example. Similarly, such lesbian scholars in the United States as Adrienne Rich condemned the heterosexual bias in women's studies that erased or miswrote lesbian experience.[79] Scholars outside the United States argued that American scholarship had to grasp the particularities of other nations and other regions, a view forcefully voiced in 1976 at a major conference on women and national development organized by the Wellesley Center for Research on Women. Among those particularities was the effect of colonial and

41

neocolonial practices and structures on Third World countries. As a Kenyan scholar who attended the Wellesley conference wrote, the study of African women means understanding

> ... economic and political relationships through which our peoples have found themselves increasingly involved with metropolitan Europe ... and the United States of America.[80]

An important result of these demands for specificity was a decrease in naive global assertions of women's commonality.

Women's Studies Today:
Achievements and
Challenges

Women's studies has changed the intellectual landscape of many traditional disciplines. Again and again, programs pass internal evaluation and review. Practitioners and texts have won conventional badges of success: grants, prizes, awards, and publication in appropriate journals. Its ideas have shaped individual minds within the classroom and outside. In 1982 a teacher in a women's studies class that was mostly black and Hispanic said her students gained "an analysis of their lives which enriches and gives a context to their intuitive convictions. Suddenly what they knew is given legitimacy, the relief of meaning, a direction for continued struggle."[81] That same year Wayne C. Booth, the internationally known literary critic, analyzed the works of Rabelais and the great literary critic Bakhtin from a feminist perspective and concluded:

> I finally accept what many feminist critics have been saying all along. Our various canons have been established by men, reading books written mostly by men for men, with women as eavesdroppers.[82]

Women's studies has also helped change public policy. Perhaps the most dramatic changes in the United States have occurred over the issues of rape, incest, pregnancy, female-headed families, and the relation of work to family life. In each issue, research uncovered a problem more serious than people had assumed.

The benefits of the new scholarship about women have been scattered widely. Feminist architectural historians in the 1970s resurrected housing plans that showed how women's domestic labor could be deprivatized and made communal. Their work became part of a Women and Housing Seminar at Hunter College in the early 1980s that brought together academics, policy makers, and housing specialists. The Center for the American Woman and Politics of Rutgers University prepared a fact sheet documenting a paucity of women on state boards and commissions that led state officials to add women to those bodies.[83] Research about the ways in which women spent their time became a basis for policy studies that showed that the United States could not achieve equal opportunity for women until they had access to child-care facilities.[84]

Despite the importance of integrating scholarship, social policy, and action, research should not be limited to that which promises purely practical results. One of the primary obligations of research is to stimulate inquiry, to ask new questions, and to think about ill-formed, inchoate subjects even when concrete gains seem inconceivable. Universities and research centers can seem slow, abstract, and fussy, but people should not judge them contemptuously for attributes that merely reflect a healthy respect for reality. Always to seek quick, pragmatic results is to risk flattening the world.

Because of the comparatively low status of the contemporary humanities, a preference for research that quickly feeds action may relegate studies of culture and the arts to the margins of interest. Such "pragmatism" fails to recognize culture's dual role. On the one hand, culture may perpetuate the devaluation of women, limiting "women's earnings and productive activities" through "direct prohibitions such as restrictions codified in religious teaching" or "through attitudes, tradition, and custom."[85] On the other hand, cultural institutions can be a spur to change. In the United States, for example, women are now entering the ministry and rabbinate in greater numbers. As they do so, they push a conservative field into a recognition of the ways in which gender bias has shaped religious institutions and symbols and into an appreciation of women's spiritual experience.[86] That field, as it alters, will help its followers to do so as well.

International Achievements

Although this publication is concerned with women's studies in the United States, women's studies has emerged vigorously in Europe and in developing countries throughout the world. Women's programs appeared in the Caribbean, Peru, Argentina, Mexico, Uruguay, Brazil, India, Thailand, Bangladesh, Korea, Japan, Australia, and other countries in the 1970s. The United Nations meetings for the International Decade for the Advancement of Women—the first in Mexico City in 1975, the second in Copenhagen in 1980, and the third in Nairobi in 1985—accelerated the process. Preparing for the Copenhagen gathering, a UNESCO-sponsored committee of experts concluded:

> . . . we recommend that UNESCO cooperate in the creation and development of both women's studies programmes and research as part of university curricula and in other relevant institutions. . . . Women in general have suffered from injustice and from traditions that have hindered their full . . . potential. . . . Programs for teaching and research in women's studies are one of the means to securing women's complete equality.[87]

Many structures of scholarship now exist in these countries: institutes, programs, networks, national and regional associations, publications, conferences, seminars, and courses; but their forms and foci, shaped as they are by local and regional conditions, differ from women's studies programs in the United States. In developing countries where poverty is so vast, women's studies must investigate literacy as well as higher education, rice-milling technologies as well as household appliances, water supplies as well as information retrieval. As a result, projects often tie research to social action. Though many researchers in the West also link the two, research on women in developing countries, according to Line Robillard Heyniger, "is seen as an integral component of a three-part global phenomenon consisting of research, social action, and grass-roots women's groups, each component reinforcing and in constant interaction with the other."[88]

The political and cultural obstacles that women's studies practitioners confront in many foreign countries are harder to surmount than in the United States. Many people in developing countries have regarded feminism or women's liberation as Western distractions. International or foreign funding agencies are often sexist in their priorities and programs. Women's bureaus, when they exist, have often provided support to women's projects and organizations, but may be unresponsive to newly defined women's issues. Certain topics are subject to censorship because they are too sensitive. A recent seminar in the Caribbean, for example, spoke of the "need to break through the repressive silencing of discussions on sexuality."[89] National and international politics threaten to divide women. In Montreal in 1982, a group of Haitian women in exile protested the listed presence of Marie-Camelle Lafontant, the director of the Haitian Research Center for the Promotion of Women and an ally of the Duvalier regimes. The terrible tensions of the Middle East have been reflected in several major conferences, including the 1980 World Conference of the United Nations Decade for Women in Copenhagen.

Women's studies in the United States has much to learn from women's studies in other countries. Challenging our affluent provincialism, international women's studies teaches us how varied women's lives have been and are. It describes societies with "varying degrees of sexual egalitarianism" and matrilineal practices.[90] It offers approaches

46

that the United States has not yet tried to such policy questions as child care, to social and political issues such as the most effective forms of women's collective action, and to such methodological concerns as the nature of "participatory research."[91] Properly done, participatory research enables women who have been excluded from power and knowledge to gain new power through knowledge. As they engage in this process, they strip away a false sense of self that dominant institutions have imposed upon them. Consistently taking her conclusions back to her subjects for verification and use, the researcher is less an "expert" than a "facilitator."[92] In São Paulo, Brazil, women from the Carlos Chagas Foundation worked with a mothers' club to construct a "collective knowledge about sexuality, such that all participants would have immediate access to that knowledge."[93] Together they produced a number of popular booklets about the female body, reproduction, and sexuality.

The United States has the most extensive women's studies resources in the world—scholars, books, journals, libraries, archives, programs, and centers. Women's studies researchers travel here from many countries. Unfortunately, not every scholar, activist, or policy maker comes to the United States in a structured program. In 1982, the Wellesley Center estimated that each year some seventy unexpected visitors arrived wanting counsel.

The lack of systematic exchange between women's studies practitioners in the United States and elsewhere is part of a larger concern: the absence of a regular, accurate international index of ongoing research, research and action projects, and women's educational programs. Such a resource, listing what has been done, could give a much needed coherence to the international research effort. Given the immense diversity of women's lives, the number of socially and intellectually important questions is enormous. Among the most pressing issues are: how have women met the basic survival needs—food and water—that have been their traditional responsibility; women and poverty; female-headed households; domestic violence; the shift from the home to the community as a provider of domestic services; the possible convergence of First and Third World women in the labor force in the global economy; education as a source of mobility and gender equality; and, finally, the impact of rapid social changes on men and women.

Opposition to Women's Studies

In the late 1960s and early 1970s opposition to women's studies took the form of ridicule and indifference. Behind both were a nexus of motives, some of them psychological in origin. Students thought the new scholarship about women might be "overwhelming, threatening, too far out." Both students and faculty, long accustomed to the cultural devaluation of women, considered women and gender unworthy of inquiry. Others argued that too many subjects were struggling for a "place in the curriculum."[94] Still others called women's studies too ideological or political, a subverter of academic standards, intellectual merit, and objectivity.

In the 1970s antagonism to women's studies was expressed through tenure and budget decisions. There was a marked reluctance to give tenure to people who specialized in women's studies. Such people could teach but they rarely became permanent members of the university community. Several prominent scholars lost their tenure cases; others won only after protracted struggles within the university or in court. In 1981 a U.S. Court of Appeals in California ruled that downgrading women's studies in a tenure decision was an indication of sex discrimination.[95] Opposition was also manifested in program cuts that were justified by institutions as financially necessary. Where the institution's fiscal problems are real, women's studies must inevitably shrink, along with everything else. However, successful campaigns have been mounted to restore arbitrarily reduced budgets to their previous dimensions.

In this decade, women's studies confronts two new developments. Now that it has proved itself as a scholarly enterprise, it has lost its reputation in some funding and publishing circles for being new and innovative. Once accused of being "faddish," women's studies is now "passé." Meanwhile, the election of Ronald Reagan in 1980 strengthened conservative forces that opposed feminism on ideological grounds and, by extension, women's studies as a "feminist invasion" of the college campus.

The conservative presence on the federal landscape has seriously affected funding for women's studies. During the 1970s federal funds for programs were critical. The Women's Educational Equity Act (WEEA) office, established in 1974 under the sponsorship of Senator Walter F. Mondale and Representative Patsy Mink, promoted equality in education and attended to the needs of racial and ethnic minority women as well as those of the handicapped. The Commission on New Funding Priorities, sponsored by the National Council for Research on Women, has documented a decline in federal support in the 1980s in its report, "A Declining Federal Commitment to Research About Women, 1980–1984" (August 1985). Funding for programs on women at the National Endowment for the Humanities has declined by almost 50 percent since Ronald Reagan took office. Mary Rubin notes that NEH funding for women's projects in fiscal year 1981, which was appropriated in October 1980, was $1,897,000, whereas funding for fiscal year 1983 was only $876,000. At the National Institute of Education, the decline was even sharper, falling from $572,000 for FY81 to $168,000 for FY83.[96]

To be sure, federal support has not entirely disappeared. In October 1982 the Committee on Equal Opportunity in Science and Technology of the National Science Foundation (NSF) stated that "elimination of funding for the re-entry program [for women who had begun careers in science and engineering] is a step backwards."[97] In 1983, NSF sponsored a visiting professor program for women in science and engineering. Nonetheless, Washington is less receptive to women's studies than it had been in 1980. Since spring 1982 the WEEA office has been the target of persistent efforts to alter it. Dr. Leslie Wolfe, who had been its director, is no longer in government; its funding has been threatened, and its staff has been reduced.[98]

Outside Washington, initiatives against women's studies both feed and are fed by the political climate in Washington. Some faculty members and administrators who were quiescent in the 1970s now are overtly hostile. In California, a group of conservative Christians, with support from state legislators, pressured the administration of California State University at Long Beach to review a women's studies program on the ground that it was promoting lesbianism. A professor was dismissed, a class canceled, and the women's center closed. In a countermove, groups filed suits to reverse these actions.[99] Some serious intellectual magazines portray women's studies as rich in ideology and political power, but poor in intellect. An essay in *Commentary* likens women's studies to an amalgam of Jezebel and the human potential movement:

> In . . . "Women's Studies" . . . feminists have left their stamp most clearly in the academy. Typically, they want it both ways: to win the game while playing by their own rules. They complain that discrimination has barred them from the rigorous, prestigious disciplines, yet given a free hand and lavish funds by cooperative administrators, they have so far produced mainly a lot of consciousness-raising and pep talks for personal growth.[100]

In sum, women's studies, which began as a counterforce and then became a force, has now provoked a second, if smaller, counterforce. At the same time, women's studies must cope with the financial scarcities of higher education today.

Mainstreaming

Women's studies practitioners have long been concerned that the field's growth along the margins of academia might relegate it to peripheral intellectual status. Because women's studies educators believe that the field is more than just a subject, that it is, in fact, a methodological and substantive perspective that challenges the premises and conclusions of other fields, they have pressed to incorporate women's studies into other disciplines.

"Mainstreaming," the effort to integrate the subject of women and the substance of women's studies into the curriculum, is a key issue to resolve in the 1980s. Mainstreaming means more than one reference to a powerful woman, more than a mention of Eleanor Roosevelt in a United States history course, more than one course in a department about women, more than a women's division in an association, more than one panel at a conference, more than one article in a scholarly journal. Mainstreaming entails the full inclusion of women's studies materials in all research, scholarship, and teaching. Should this take place, proponents argue, it would transform the curriculum.

The range of mainstreaming activities is impressive. On a local, regional, and national level, faculty development projects are effective devices for mainstreaming. Faculty members may get released time or stipends to learn the new approaches and materials of women's studies. Notable efforts include: the Wellesley Center's program of seminars, fellowships, a national consulting program, and a directory of projects, all started in 1977; summer institutes in women's history for high school teachers given by the Committee on Women Historians of the American Historical Association in 1977 and 1978; and a summer institute, "Women's Nontraditional Literature: Theory and Practice," organized by the Modern Language Association at the University of Alabama in 1979. The purpose of the MLA institute was to "equip literary scholars . . . to use nontraditional materials." *Nontraditional* refers to materials excluded from the "standard canon": forgotten published literature, private genres such as letters and diaries, and oral testimony.[101]

In 1980–1981 Wheaton College undertook a three-year revision of its introductory courses in order to bring the study of women into the core liberal arts curriculum. In 1981 the Yale Women's Studies program sponsored a faculty development seminar. In 1981 Barbara Haber at the Schlesinger Library organized a project that brought seven teams to Radcliffe College to work on women's studies programming in local public libraries. She received ninety-five completed applications from forty-seven states and the Virgin Islands for the available places. In 1983 Hunter College held its first workshop to integrate the subject of women, department by department, into introductory courses. In 1983, too, the Organization of American Historians published the first of four "teaching packets" for fusing women's history into survey courses on Western civilization and United States history in order to make possible ". . . a better survey, not a course in women's history."[102]

Supplementing mainstreaming are two related activities: dissemination and outreach. Both aim at making women's studies accessible beyond the academic community. Dissemination implies efforts to speak to influential publics; outreach, a homelier term, suggests building bridges between women's studies and the community. Successful projects require an accurate assessment of an audience's needs and interest, careful planning with representation from the target audiences, and translation of obscure or jargon-filled academic prose into ordinary discourse.

Mainstreaming is essential and overdue. Women's studies can add significantly not only to the liberal arts but also to courses in agricultural, business, and professional schools, and in colleges of education. However, it also raises serious questions. First, the mainstreaming metaphor itself. Peggy McIntosh at the Wellesley Center believes that the metaphor trivializes women by implying that women have not been part of the central flow of life. More significantly, the metaphor suggests that feminist scholarship is a tributary which will merge into the main river. Properly understood, however, feminist scholarship should rechannel the river.[103] Others suspect that the theory of mainstreaming will be easily corrupted in practice. A faculty member can go about his or her ordinary business, pausing only to host the occasional "ladies' day." A church historian might speak for twelve weeks about prominent clergymen, and then, for one week, trot out a few great women.[104] Still others fear that mainstreaming will destroy the political and intellectual power of women's studies. Distinguishing "integrationists" from "advocates of autonomous women's studies" are the following claims:

> ... the integrationists hope to achieve the transformation from within the very framework which we believe needs transforming ...

In contrast, women's studies offers a new frame:

> ... in which women's different and differing ideas, experiences, needs and interests are valid in their own right and form the basis for our teaching and learning.[105]

At present, women's studies seems to need *both* its own courses *and* extensive mainstreaming projects. They are mutually supportive efforts. Women's studies is the fount of mainstreaming endeavors. Neglect of women's studies would dry up the sources of mainstreaming—women's studies courses and their practitioners.[106] Simultaneously, disdain of mainstreaming risks quasi-permanent marginalization.

The women's studies movement is correct in wanting its own independent structures, such as research centers, and the incorporation of its goals within less women-specific structures. Like feminism, women's studies has had at least two goals: autonomy for women, which independent structures promote and symbolize, and equity between men and women, which can only be achieved in the larger universe in which they both live. Indeed, autonomy is a precondition of equity. For its long-term health, women's studies needs a fission process, in which it creates institutions, and a fusion process, in which it moves toward other groups. The two processes have complementary, not competing, virtues. The first, for example, may be much more supportive of explicitly feminist activity and ideas. The second engages the world that is to be transformed.

The Future of
Women's Studies

In the United States, women's studies is in a middle period,
a time of consolidation that is neither monolithic nor uni-
form. The diversity apparent since 1969 remains. In some
institutions—UCLA and Rutgers, for example—programs
are growing. In other institutions student enrollments have
stabilized or declined. In 1983 at the University of Oregon
enrollments were down—in part because of student perceptions that women's problems were solved and that wom-
en's studies was not very helpful in preparing for a career.
However, women in the Oregon community remain supportive, and the women's research center is fiscally sound.

Women's studies must accept the likelihood that enrollments will periodically and temporarily decline, particularly during periods when students are preoccupied with
career goals. Women's studies programs might offer two
kinds of courses: one to introduce students to the history
of gender, to the study of sex roles, and to theories of gender equality; and a second to instruct students who are
already familiar with these issues and wish to go more
deeply into them. In the late 1960s and 1970s the latter
group often prodded faculty outside of women's studies to

include its material in their lectures and reading lists. Clearly, if a women's studies program is to offer a significant number of courses, it must appeal to a wide variety of students. However, the argument for a program ought not to rest on student interest and enrollment alone. It should also spring from a desire to be of general service to a college or university.

Among the most substantial of those services is research. A new generation of scholars is moving from articles, which present an argument, to books, which address broader perspectives. The past decade has also accumulated an immense amount of knowledge, "a critical mass of monographic material," which is the base for the construction of large ideas and theories.[107] Hard questions continue to demand the accumulation of facts and the construction of theory. The intellectual agenda of women's studies now includes: (1) brain organization and sex differences in cognition; (2) the ways in which we perceive differences among people—between sexes, among races, across classes, across generations—and ways in which we then organize those perceptions into psychological patterns and social structures built on domination and submission, superiority and inferiority, violence and victimization; (3) motherhood and child care; (4) the feminization of poverty; (5) equal pay for work of comparable worth; (6) the conditions that lead to gender change and the relationship of change to equality; and (7) feminist theory and its connections to other philosophical and political concepts.

The future of women's studies will depend on its ability to respond to the needs of this middle period. A first step should be a rigorous self-assessment to ascertain the scope of women's studies. Exactly how many courses, programs, and centers are there? What is the life expectancy of a course within a department or within a women's studies program? What are the measurable long-term effects of mainstreaming projects? What is the relationship of women's studies to the politics of the 1980s? How significant is ideologically conservative opposition? Do block educational grants to states exclude or include women's projects and women's studies?

In addition, women's studies has to reach out to still more constituencies. In doing so, it will increase the diversity that has been its intellectual and institutional strength. For example, more should be done with primary and secondary schools, and with junior and community colleges. Women outnumber men at community colleges, and many are disadvantaged, with acute economic needs, family responsibilities, and limited skills.[108] Some community colleges have women's studies programs and resources, but much more needs to be done.

Another important new constituency is the generation of women now in their twenties. The generation that started women's studies in the United States is now, for the most part, middle-aged. It had *élan*, but only a few historical precedents to imitate. Younger women now have the founders as a precedent. Unfortunately, the founders have not thought enough about the role of their successors. They have not asked how students (female and male), trained in the women's studies programs the founders created, may themselves now act as leaders.[109] To be sure, graduate student interest is there. Recently, four out of the five top female applicants for graduate study in American history at Stanford University wanted to study women's history.[110] Ironically, the first generation's training programs and pressure have helped bring about more opportunities in educational administration for younger women who can now ignore "women's jobs" in favor of "the real action." Both scholars and administrators may mistakenly think of themselves as "post-feminists" to whom the politics of their "mothers" is irrelevant, even embarrassing.

Women's studies cannot control the circumstances needed for its survival. A haunting problem is that of faculty stability, which is essential to provide continuity and intellectual maturity. Part-timers interested in women's studies have underpaid, marginal positions. Junior faculty leave—sometimes because they want to, more often because they must. "I am," says Myra Strober, director of the Stanford Center for Research on Women, "remarkably impressed with how ineffective we have been in getting permanent faculty."[111]

At least three causes promote faculty instability: (1) Tenure has become much more difficult to achieve in American colleges and universities. (2) A stigma is still imprinted on women's studies because it is comparatively new, because it has interdisciplinary ambitions, because it deals with women, and because of its historical connections to feminism. (3) Most women's studies programs depend for their staff on joint appointments with other departments. Separate tenure lines in women's studies, or in the study of women in a discipline, would give a program legitimacy, predictability, a degree of autonomy, and a base from which to work within a college or university. Yet only a handful of schools have such lines—among them California State University/San Diego, the University of Wisconsin/Madison, Barnard College, and Douglass College/Rutgers University.

Finally, the national network of women's research centers must diversify sources of financial support in order to continue. This entails developing as many sources of funding as possible: the community and state, grants, contracts, endowment, and university program support. Indeed, outside funders of the university research centers might look first at the degree of underwriting a center has from its own institution in order to avoid piling soft monies on top of soft monies as if they were scoops in an ice cream cone. In order to attract support, each center will have to assess and strengthen its program. There must be a balance between its basic research and its ability to integrate research with policy. Although flexibility is important, each center should have a sharp focus as the core of its identity. Only if each center has its own well-defined and articulated tasks can the centers as a group avoid redundancies that offer the illusion, but not the reality, of activity.

The reconstruction of gender relations—in thought, daily life, social and economic structures, and culture—is rough, asymmetrical, disorderly in pace and consequence. Lacking the smoothness of the Newtonian world, it is perhaps the equivalent of the pulsations of quanta in the post-Einsteinian world. The responsibility of women's studies is to reveal, richly and accurately, how men and women have lived, how the fact that they have been men or women has mattered, and how gender relations are constructed and reconstructed. The passion of women's studies is to insist that old dreams of a balance between freedom and community, between autonomy and equality, for both men and women, have a new vitality and vision.

In the United States, women's studies, like the contemporary reconstruction of gender relations, is under way. It has far surpassed its origins. It may not yet have achieved a full public understanding of its purpose and capabilities, its growth and significance, but its direction is clear—toward nothing less than a new architecture of consciousness and culture.

Notes

1. "The American Scholar," in *The Complete Essays and Other Writings of Ralph Waldo Emerson*, ed. Brooks Atkinson, New York: Modern Library, 1950, page 55.

2. "Woman in the Nineteenth Century," in *The Woman and the Myth: Margaret Fuller's Life and Writings*, ed. Bell Gale Chevigny, Old Westbury, N.Y.: Feminist Press, 1976, page 248.

3. *The American Mind,* New Haven: Yale University Press, 1950, page 10.

4. Twelfth Annual Report of the Board of Education, 1848 (Boston, 1849), page 59.

5. Laurence Veysey, *The Emergence of the American University,* Chicago: University of Chicago Press, 1965, p. 28.

6. Frederick Rudolph, *Curriculum: A History of the American Undergraduate Course of Study Since 1636,* San Francisco: Jossey-Bass Publishers, 1978, page 58.

7. *Ibid.,* pages 63-103.

8. Ed. Sheila Tobias, Pittsburgh: KNOW, Inc., 1970.

9. Florence Howe, "The Power of Education," in *Women's Studies and the Curriculum,* Winston-Salem, N.C.: Salem College, 1983, page 24.

10. Marilyn Boxer, "Review Essay: For and About Women: The Theory and Practice of Women's Studies in the United States," *Signs* 7, 3 (Spring 1982), page 662.

11. Florence Howe, *Seven Years Later: Women's Studies Programs in 1976*, Washington, D.C.: National Advisory Council on Women's Educational Programs, 1977.

12. Jane Williamson, *New Feminist Scholarship: A Guide to Bibliographies*, Old Westbury, N.Y.: Feminist Press, 1979; Patricia K. Ballou, *Women: A Bibliography of Bibliographies*, Boston: G. K. Hall, 1980, which Ballou is now revising and updating.

13. Nina Cobb, "Letter from Poughkeepsie," *RF Illustrated* (publication of the Rockefeller Foundation), November 1981, page 3.

14. Florence Howe and Paul Lauter, *The Impact of Women's Studies on the Campus and the Disciplines*, Washington, D.C.: U.S. Department of Health, Education and Welfare, National Institute of Education, 1980, pages 40-44. See also Catharine R. Stimpson, "The New Scholarship about Women: The State of the Art," *Annals of Scholarship* I (Spring 1980), pages 2-14.

15. Patricia Albjerg Graham, "Women in Higher Education," *Signs* III, 4 (Summer 1978), page 764.

16. Michael J. Carter and Susan Boslego Carter, "Women's Recent Progress in the Professions or, Women Get a Ticket to Ride After the Gravy Train Has Left the Station," *Feminist Studies* VII (Fall 1981), page 480. See also William Chafe, *The American Woman: Her Changing Social, Economic and Political Roles, 1920-70*, New York: Oxford University Press, 1974, pages 93-94.

17. Jo Freeman, "Women on the Move: The Roots of Revolt," in *Women on the Move*, ed. Alice S. Rossi and Ann Calderwood, New York: Russell Sage, 1973, page 1.

18. Joyce Antler, "Culture, Service, and Work: Changing Ideals of Higher Education for Women," in *The Undergraduate Woman: Issues in Educational Equity*, ed. Pamela Perun, Lexington, Mass.: Lexington Books, 1982, p. 29.

19. Chafe, *The American Woman*, page 208.

20. Anne Kimbell Relph, "The World Center for Women's Archives," *Signs* IV, 3 (Spring 1979), pages 597-603; Linda J. Henry, "Promoting Historical Consciousness: The Early Archives Committee on the National Council of Negro Women," *Signs* 7, 1 (Autumn 1981), pages 251-59.

21. Rosalind Rosenberg, *Beyond Separate Spheres: Intellectual Roots of Modern Feminism,* New Haven: Yale University Press, 1982, page 234.

22. Florence Howe, "Interpreting Women's Education: Liberation or Social Control?" transcript of *Women and Education in America: The Last 150 Years,* symposium at Mt. Holyoke College, April 1982, ed. John M. Faragher, page 13.

23. Rosenberg, *Beyond Separate Spheres,* pages 238-46.

24. Quotations from Nannerl Keohane, "Women's Education and Feminism," *Women and Education in America,* pages 107-108.

25. Jean W. Campbell, "Nontraditional Student in Academe," in *Women in Higher Education,* ed. W. Todd Furniss and Patricia Albjerg Graham, Washington, D.C.: American Council on Education, 1974, page 192.

26. Sara Evans, *Personal Politics: The Roots of Women's Liberation in the Civil Rights Movement and the New Left,* New York: Alfred A. Knopf, 1979, page 24. Much of my analysis here is from Evans.

27. *Female Studies* No. 2, ed. Florence Howe and Carol Ahlum, Pittsburgh, Pa.: KNOW, Inc., 1970, pages 1-2.

28. Alice Kessler-Harris, *Out to Work: A History of Wage-Earning Women in the United States,* New York: Oxford University Press, 1982, page 302.

29. *Ibid.,* page 301.

30. Howe and Ahlum, "Women's Studies and Social Change," *Academic Women on the Move,* page 395.

31. Dorothy E. Smith, "A Sociology for Women," in *The Prism of Sex: Essays in the Sociology of Knowledge,* ed. Julia A. Sherman and Evelyn Torton Beck, Madison: University of Wisconsin Press, 1977, page 136.

32. Marilyn Salzman-Webb, "Program Description, Goddard College," *Female Studies* No. 3, ed. Florence Howe and Carol Ahlum, Pittsburgh: KNOW, Inc., 1971, pages 156-57.

33. Mary Parlee, "Review Essay: Psychology," *Signs* I, 1 (Autumn 1975), pages 121-22.

34. Margaret Jones Bolsterli, "Teaching Women's Studies at the University of Arkansas," *Stepping Off the Pedestal: Academic Women in the South,* ed. Patricia A. Stringer and Irene

Thompson, New York: Modern Language Association, 1982, page 72.

35. Rosabeth Moss Kanter, *Men and Women of the Corporation*, New York: Basic Books, 1977, page xi.

36. Florence Howe, Introduction to special issue on "Women and Education," *Harvard Educational Review* (November 1979), page 415.

37. Carl Degler, "Charlotte Anna Perkins Stetson Gilman," *Notable American Women* Vol. II, Cambridge, Mass.: Belknap Press of Harvard University Press, 1971, page 40.

38. Introduction to *Women and Economics*, New York: Harper & Row (Torchbook edition), 1966, pages vi-viii.

39. Personal interview, Washington, D.C., Nov. 5, 1982. See also Diana Pearce and Harriette McAdoo, *Women and Children: Alone and in Poverty*, Washington, D.C.: National Advisory Council on Economic Opportunity, 1981.

40. Barbara Sicherman, E. William Monter, Joan Wallach Scott, and Kathryn Kish Sklar, *Recent United States Scholarship in the History of Women*, Washington, D.C.: American Historical Association, 1980, page 1.

41. Anne Firor Scott, "On Seeing and Not Seeing: A Case of Historical Invisibility," *Journal of American History* (June 1984), pages 7-21. Also personal interview with Anne F. Scott, February 1985.

42. *Academic Women*, Cleveland: World Publishing, 1964, paperback, 1966, page ix.

43. Evans, *Personal Politics*, page ix.

44. In one of Catharine Stimpson's courses at Douglass College/Rutgers University, English Department.

45. Boxer, "Review Essay," page 665.

46. Howe and Lauter, *Impact of Women's Studies*, page 29.

47. Nina Cobb, "The Schlesinger Library," *RF Illustrated*, December 1983, page 5.

48. *Financial Support of Women's Programs in the 1970s: A Review of Private and Government Funding in the United States and Abroad*, New York: Ford Foundation, 1979.

49. Personal interview with Margaret B. Wilkerson, director, University of California (Berkeley) Center for Study, Education and Advancement of Women, September 7, 1982.

50. Telephone interview, Professor Joan Acker, director, September 24, 1983.

51. Mariam Chamberlain, "A Period of Remarkable Growth: Women's Studies Research Centers," *Change* XIV (April 1982), page 24.

52. The Bunting Institute did the survey. In July 1981, the Women's Research and Education Institute isolated, in "A Directory of Selected Women's Research and Policy Centers," thirty-eight "research foci" in the twenty centers it surveyed.

53. *Newsletter,* Number 13 (October 1982).

54. Personal interview with Ruth B. Mandel, director, Center for the American Woman and Politics, Rutgers University, October 5, 1982.

55. "Annual Report 1980-81," Wellesley College Center for Research on Women, Wellesley, Massachusetts, January 1982, page 23.

56. Virginia Cyrus, "Report from the Chair of the Steering Committee," *National Women's Studies Association Newsletter* I (Spring 1983).

57. "Introduction: Teaching about Women, 1971," *Female Studies IV: Teaching About Women,* Pittsburgh: KNOW, Inc., 1971, page ii.

58. "Women's Studies: Renaissance or Revolution?" in *Women's Studies: An Interdisciplinary Journal* III (1976), pages 122-23.

59. *AWIS Newsletter* XX, 4, page 4.

60. Helen S. Astin and Mary Beth Snyder, "Affirmative Action 1972-1982: A Decade of Response," *Change* (July-August 1982), pages 26-31, 59.

61. Carter and Carter, "Women's Recent Progress in the Professions," page 480.

62. "Theorising about Theorising," *Theories of Women's Studies,* ed. Gloria Bowles and Renate Duelli Klein, London and Boston: Routledge & Kegan Paul, 1983, page 28.

63. Dorothy Smith, "A Sociology for Women," page 169.

64. Gilligan, page 19, my italics.

65. Smith-Rosenberg, "The Feminist Reconstruction of History," *Academe* LXIX (September-October 1983), page 28.

66. Gayle Rubin, "The Traffic in Women: Notes on the 'Political Economy' of Sex," in *Towards an Anthropology of Women,* ed. Rayna Rapp Reiter, New York: Monthly Review Press, 1975, pages 157-210.

67. "Feminism and Economics," *Academe* LXIX (September-October 1983), page 22.

68. Jeanne Dost, "Women [sic] Studies Thrives at Oregon State University," *Northwest Women's Report* II (January-February 1983), page 1.

69. Marcia Westkott, "Women's Studies as a Strategy for Change," *Theories of Women's Studies,* page 213.

70. Adrienne Germain, *Poor Rural Women: A Policy Perspective,* Ford Foundation reprint from *Journal of International Affairs* 30, 2 (Fall-Winter, 1976-77), pages 13-14.

71. Estelle Freedman, "Separatism as Strategy: Female Institution Building and American Feminism, 1870-1930," in *Feminist Studies* V (Fall 1979), pages 512-29. See, too, Martha Vicinus, *Independent Women,* Chicago: University of Chicago Press, 1985.

72. Alice Kessler-Harris, *Out to Work,* New York: Oxford University Press, 1982; Cynthia Fuchs Epstein, *Women in Law,* New York: Basic Books, 1981; Judith H. Stiehm, *Bring Me Men and Women: Mandated Change at the U.S. Air Force Academy,* Berkeley: University of California Press, 1981; Elaine Showalter, *A Literature of Their Own,* Princeton: Princeton University Press, 1977; Jeane J. Kirkpatrick, *Political Women,* New York: Basic Books, 1974. This list is representative, not inclusive.

73. Nancy Chodorow, *The Reproduction of Mothering: Psychoanalysis and the Sociology of Gender,* Berkeley: University of California Press, 1978.

74. "The Economics of Divorce: Social and Economic Consequences of Property, Alimony and Child Support Awards," *UCLA Law Review* XXVIII (August 1981), page 1266.

75. Cynthia Fuchs Epstein, "Ideal Images and Real Roles: The Perpetuation of Gender Inequality," *Dissent,* 31 (Fall 1984), page 441.

76. Rossi, "A Biosocial Perspective on Parenting," *Daedalus* (Spring 1977), pages 1-33. For comment, see *Signs* IV, 4 (Summer 1979), pages 695-717.

77. Mary Hartman, "Capitalism and the Sexes" (rev. of Julie A. Matthaei, *An Economic History of Women*), *Raritan Review*, 4, 1 (Summer 1984), page 133.

78. Bonnie Thornton Dill, director, Memphis State University Center for Research on Women, personal interview, San Francisco, September 7, 1982, notes how greatly the study of the interaction of race, class, and gender alters the study of gender.

79. Adrienne Rich, "Compulsory Heterosexuality and Lesbian Existences," *Signs* V, 4 (Summer 1980), pages 631-60.

80. Achola O. Pala, "Definitions of Women and Development: An African Perspective," *The Black Woman Cross-Culturally*, ed. Filomina Chioma Steady, Cambridge: Schenkman Publishing, 1981, page 209.

81. Jane Lazarre, "Restoring Lives at City College," *Village Voice*, May 18, 1982, page 14. A Ford Foundation paper, "Women's Program Review, January 1981," notes that those union women who take women's studies courses are apt to become more active and to seek additional education.

82. Wayne C. Booth, "Freedom of Interpretation: Bakhtin and the Challenge of Feminist Criticism," *Critical Inquiry* IX (September 1982), page 74.

83. Mandel interview cited in note 54.

84. Personal interviews with Laura Lein, director, Peggy McIntosh, and Joseph Pleck, at the Wellesley College Center for Research on Women, October 29, 1982. Jean Baker Miller, director, Stone Center for Developmental Services and Studies, was also present. Lein and Pleck, with James A. Levine, Sharon Harlan, and Michelle Seligson, co-authored *Child Care and Equal Opportunities for Women*, Washington, D.C.: United States Commission On Civil Rights, Clearinghouse Publication No. 67, June 1981.

85. *Women in the World*, New York: Ford Foundation, November 1980, page 22.

86. Personal interview with Constance Buchanan, director, Women's Studies Program, Harvard Divinity School, and George Rupp, then dean, Harvard Divinity School, at the Divinity School, Cambridge, Mass., November 5, 1982.

87. "A Final Report and Recommendations," Meeting of Experts on Research and Teaching Related to Women, Paris:

UNESCO, 5-8 May 1980, page 1.

88. Line Robillard Heyniger, "Women Researching Women," *IDRC Reports* XII (April 1983), page 19. See also pre-conference papers from the International Conference on Research and Teaching Related to Women, Simone de Beauvoir Institute, Concordia University, Montreal, Canada, July 26–August 4, 1982.

89. Kate Young and Marcia Rivera Quintero, *Women and Social Production in the Caribbean,* final report of seminar sponsored by IDS and CEREP, San Juan, Puerto Rico: IDS/CEREP, 1982, page 42.

90. *Black Woman Cross-Culturally,* ed. Steady, page 2 (note 80).

91. In a personal interview on November 5, 1982, Isabel Nieves, International Center for Research on Women, Washington, D.C., cautioned against too glib a use of the phrase.

92. Teresita Quinto Deles, Filipino Kapipapan Ng Kababai-hang, plenary session Montreal conference, August 4, 1982.

93. Cristina Bruschini, Carmen Barroso, Cecilia Simonetti, and Elizabeth Meloni, "Walking Together: Sex Education in the Periphery of São Paulo," unpublished manuscript, page 7.

94. Quotes from Alice F. Emerson, "Current Challenges for the Education of Women," *Women Studies Quarterly* X (Spring 1982), page 4.

95. *Lynn* v. *University of California,* U.S. Court of Appeals, Ninth Circuit (San Francisco) No. 79-3384, September 21, 1981.

96. Telephone interview, Mary Rubin, National Council for Research on Women, June 27, 1985. These figures for obligated funds for projects about women have been adjusted by Rubin. Figures for FY84 still need analysis. The total budgets for NIE were $65 million for FY81 and $53 million for FY83.

97. *Annual Report,* page 20.

98. "The Impact of the 1982 Federal Budget on Women in Higher Education," *Academe* LXVII (August 1981), pages 202-204; *Peer Perspective* VII (November 1981), pages 1, 9; *Peer Perspective* VIII (July 1982), pages 1, 8.

99. *Chronicle of Higher Education,* May 19, 1982, page 8; *New York Times,* August 6, 1982, page A-8.

66

100. "Feminism and Thought Control," *Commentary* (June 1982), page 42. See also Michael Levin, "The Feminist Mystique," *Commentary* (December 1980), pages 25-30, with correspondence in further issues; and Midge Decter, "On Affirmative Action and Lost Self-Respect," *New York Times,* July 6, 1980, page E-17.

101. Institute brochure.

102. *Restoring Women to History: Materials for Western Civilization* I, eds. Elizabeth Fox-Genovese and Susan Mosher Stuard, Bloomington, Indiana: Organization of American Historians, 1983, page 3. Dr. Myra Dinnerstein, director of the Southwest Institute for Research on Women at the University of Arizona, in correspondence and conversation, has been a helpful guide to mainstream activities.

103. "A Note on Terminology," *Women's Studies Quarterly* XI (Summer 1983), pages 29-30.

104. Rosemary Radford Ruether, "The Feminist Critique in Religious Studies," *Soundings* LXIV (Winter 1981), page 397.

105. Gloria Bowles and Renate Duelli Klein, "Introduction," *Theories of Women's Studies,* page 3.

106. Paraphrase of remarks by Joan Wallach Scott, then director, Pembroke Center, in a telephone interview, September 29, 1983.

107. Scott interview cited in note 106.

108. For detail, see Allana Elovson, *Women's Studies in the Community Colleges,* Washington, D.C.: Department of Health, Education and Welfare, National Institute of Education, 1980, 43 pages; and Mary Lou Randour, Georgia L. Strasburg and Jean Lipman-Blumen, "Research Report, Women in Higher Education: Trends in Enrollment and Degrees Earned," *Harvard Education Review,* 52, 2 (May 1982), pages 189-202.

109. Phone interview, Professor Elaine Marks, then director, University of Wisconsin, Women's Studies Research Center, November 16, 1982.

110. Carl N. Degler, "The Legitimacy of Scholarship by and about Women," *Chronicle of Higher Education,* September 15, 1982, page 56.

111. Personal interview, Palo Alto, California, September 6, 1982.

Selected Bibliography

This bibliography, compiled largely by Elsa Dixler, is necessarily selective. Focusing on the United States, it does not include important books from and about other countries. Nor does it mention fully enough the contribution of some journals, especially *Feminist Studies* and *Women's Studies,* in which influential ideas often first appeared. Instead, I have provided the titles of some significant texts to suggest the range of women's studies. The organization merges thematic and disciplinary categories. It contains a section on feminist theory, which has given women's studies some of its most provocative and powerful insights, as well as a section on literature, which scholars have used as a source on social structures, cultural patterns, language, and feelings. An earlier version of this bibliography appeared in *Ms.* (October 1983), and portions are printed here with permission.

Anthropology and Sociology

Leacock, Eleanor Burke. *Myths of Male Dominance.* New York: Monthly Review Press, 1981.

Lopata, Helena Z. *Occupation: Housewife.* 1971. Westport, Conn.: Greenwood Press, 1980.

MacCormack, Carol, and Marilyn Strathern. *Nature, Culture and Gender.* New York: Cambridge University Press, 1980.

Reiter, Rayna Rapp. *Toward an Anthropology of Women.* New York: Monthly Review Press, 1975.

Rosaldo, Michelle, and Louise Lamphere. *Women, Culture, and Society.* Stanford: Stanford University Press, 1974.

Tuchman, Gaye, Arlene Kaplan Daniels, and James Benet, eds. *Hearth and Home: Images of Women in the Mass Media.* New York: Oxford University Press, 1978.

Art and Architecture

Berger, John. *Ways of Seeing.* London: Penguin, 1977.

Birch, Eugenie Ladner, ed. *The Unsheltered Woman: Women and Housing in the 80s.* New Brunswick, N.J.: Center for Urban Policy Research, 1985.

Hayden, Dolores. *The Grand Domestic Revolution: A History of Feminist Designs for American Homes, Neighborhoods, and Cities.* Cambridge, Mass.: MIT Press, 1981.

————. *Redesigning the American Dream: The Future of Housing, Work and Family Life.* New York: W.W. Norton, 1984.

Nochlin, Linda, and Ann Sutherland Harris. *Women Artists, 1550-1950.* New York: Knopf, 1977.

Stimpson, Catharine, Elsa Dixler, Martha Nelson, and Kathryn Yatrakis, eds. *Women and the American City.* Chicago: University of Chicago Press, 1981.

Economics and Work

Howe, Louise Kapp. *Pink-Collar Workers: Inside the World of Women's Work.* New York: Putnam, 1977.

Kanter, Rosabeth Moss. *Men and Women of the Corporation.* New York: Basic Books, 1977.

Kessler-Harris, Alice. *Out to Work: A History of Wage-Earning Women in the United States.* New York: Oxford University Press, 1982.

Lloyd, Cynthia B., and Beth Niemi. *The Economics of Sex Differentials.* New York: Columbia University Press, 1980.

Sawhill, Isabel, and Heather Ross. *Time of Transition: The Growth of Families Headed by Women.* Washington, D.C.: Urban Institute, 1975.

Scott, Joan, and Louise Tilly. *Women, Work, and Family.* New York: Holt, Rinehart & Winston, 1978.

Strasser, Susan. *Never Done: A History of American Housework.* New York: Pantheon, 1982.

Wallace, Phyllis. *Black Women in the Labor Force.* Cambridge: MIT Press, 1980.

Fiction

Arnow, Harriet. *The Dollmaker*. 1954. New York: Avon Books, 1973.

Brown, Rita Mae. *Rubyfruit Jungle*. New York: Bantam Books, 1977.

Chopin, Kate. *The Awakening*. 1899. New York: Avon Books, 1972.

Eliot, George. *Middlemarch*. 1871-1874. New York: Penguin, 1965.

French, Marilyn. *The Women's Room*. New York: Summit, 1977.

Gilman, Charlotte Perkins. *The Yellow Wallpaper*. 1892. New York: Feminist Press, 1973.

————. *Herland: A Lost Feminist Utopian Novel*. 1915. New York: Pantheon, 1978.

Hurston, Zora Neale. *Their Eyes Were Watching God*. 1937. Champaign: University of Illinois Press, 1978.

Kingston, Maxine Hong. *The Woman Warrior: Memoirs of a Girlhood among Ghosts*. New York: Knopf, 1976.

Lessing, Doris. *The Golden Notebook*. New York: Simon & Schuster, 1962.

Morrison, Toni. *The Bluest Eye*. New York: Washington Square Press, 1972.

Piercy, Marge. *Small Changes*. New York: Doubleday, 1973.

Plath, Sylvia. *The Bell Jar*. New York: Harper & Row, 1971.

Walker, Alice. *Meridian*. New York: Harcourt Brace Jovanovich, 1976.

————. *The Color Purple*. New York: Harcourt Brace Jovanovich, 1982.

History

Cott, Nancy. *The Bonds of Womanhood: "Woman's Sphere" in New England, 1780-1835*. New Haven: Yale University Press, 1978.

Cott, Nancy, and Elizabeth Pleck, eds. *A Heritage of Her Own: Toward a New Social History of Women*. New York: Simon & Schuster, 1980.

Degler, Carl. *At Odds: Woman and the Family in America, from the Revolution to the Present*. New York: Oxford University Press, 1980.

Douglas, Ann. *The Feminization of American Culture.* New York: Knopf, 1978.

Gordon, Linda. *Woman's Body, Woman's Right: A Social History of Birth Control.* New York: Viking, 1976.

James, Edward T., and Janet W. James, eds. *Notable American Women, 1607- 1950: A Bibliographical Dictionary.* Volumes 1-3. Cambridge: Harvard University Press, 1971.

Kelly, Joan. *Women, History and Theory.* Chicago: University of Chicago Press, 1984.

Lerner, Gerda. *The Majority Finds Its Past: Placing Women in History.* New York: Oxford University Press, 1979.

Sicherman, Barbara, ed. *The Modern Period.* Volume 4. In *Notable American Women, 1607-1950: A Bibliographical Dictionary.* Cambridge: Harvard University Press, 1980.

Sklar, Kathryn Kish. *Catharine Beecher: A Study in American Domesticity.* New Haven: Yale University Press, 1973.

Smith-Rosenberg, Carroll. *Disorderly Conduct: Visions of Gender in Victorian America.* New York: Knopf, 1985.

Ulrich, Laurel Thatcher. *Good Wives.* New York: Knopf, 1982.

Vicinus, Martha. *Independent Women.* Chicago: University of Chicago Press, 1985.

History of Feminism

DuBois, Ellen. *Feminism and Suffrage: The Emergence of an Independent Women's Movement in America, 1848-1869.* Ithaca: Cornell University Press, 1978.

Evans, Sara. *Personal Politics: The Roots of Women's Liberation in the Civil Rights Movement and the New Left.* New York: Knopf, 1978.

Flexner, Eleanor. *Century of Struggle: The Woman's Rights Movement in the United States.* Revised edition. Cambridge, Mass.: Harvard University Press, 1975.

Literary and Film Criticism

De Lauretis, Teresa. *Alice Doesn't: Feminism, Semiotics, Cinema.* Bloomington: Indiana University Press, 1984.

Ellmann, Mary. *Thinking About Women.* New York: Harcourt Brace & World, 1968.

Faderman, Lillian. *Surpassing the Love of Men: Love Between Women from the Renaissance to the Present.* New York: Morrow, 1981.

Gilbert, Sandra M., and Susan Gubar. *The Madwoman in the Attic: The Woman Writer and the Nineteenth-Century Literary Imagination*. New Haven: Yale University Press, 1979.

———. *The Norton Anthology of Literature: The Tradition in English*. New York: W.W. Norton, 1985.

Heilbrun, Carolyn. *Toward a Recognition of Androgyny*. New York: Knopf, 1973.

Jardine, Alice A. *Gynesis*. Ithaca, N.Y.: Cornell University Press, 1985.

Olsen, Tillie. *Silences*. New York: Dell, 1979.

Radway, Janice. *Reading the Romance*. Chapel Hill: University of North Carolina Press, 1984.

Showalter, Elaine. *A Literature of Their Own: British Women Novelists from Brontë to Lessing*. Princeton: Princeton University Press, 1977.

Walker, Alice. *In Search of Our Mothers' Gardens*. New York: Harcourt Brace Jovanovich, 1983.

Woolf, Virginia. *A Room of One's Own*. 1929. New York: Harcourt Brace Jovanovich, 1963.

Motherhood

Arms, Suzanne. *Immaculate Deception: A New Look at Childbirth in America*. Boston: Houghton Mifflin, 1975.

Chodorow, Nancy. *The Reproduction of Mothering: Psychoanalysis and the Sociology of Gender*. Berkeley: University of California Press, 1978.

Dinnerstein, Dorothy. *The Mermaid and the Minotaur: Sexual Arrangements and the Human Malaise*. New York: Harper & Row, 1977.

Rich, Adrienne. *Of Woman Born: Motherhood as Experience and Institution*. New York: Norton, 1976.

Wertz, Richard, and Dorothy Wertz. *Lying-In: A History of Childbirth in America*. New York: Free Press, 1977.

Music

Block, Adrienne Fried, and Carol Neuls-Bates, eds. *Women in American Music: A Bibliography of Music and Literature*. Westport, Conn.: Greenwood Press, 1979.

Bowers, Jane, and Judith Tick, eds. *Women Making Music: The*

Western Art Tradition 1150-1950. University of Illinois Press, 1985.

Neuls-Bates, Carol, ed. *Women in Music: An Anthology of Source Readings.* New York: Harper & Row, 1982.

Politics and Law

Babcock, Barbara, Ann Freedman, Eleanor Holmes Norton, and Susan Ross. *Sex Discrimination and the Law: Causes and Remedies.* New York: Little, Brown, 1975.

Brown, Barbara, Ann Freedman, Harriet Katz, and Alice Price. *Women's Rights and the Law.* New York: Praeger, 1977.

Elshtain, Jean Bethke. *Public Man, Private Woman: Women in Social and Political Thought.* Princeton: Princeton University Press, 1981.

Freeman, Jo. *The Politics of Women's Liberation.* New York: Longman, 1975.

Jaggar, Alison M. *Feminist Politics and Human Nature.* Totowa, N.J.: Rowman and Allanheld, 1983.

Kanowitz, Leo. *Women and the Law: The Unfinished Revolution.* Albuquerque: New Mexico University Press, 1969.

Klein, Ethel. *Gender Politics.* Cambridge: Harvard University Press, 1984.

Okin, Susan. *Women in Western Political Thought.* Princeton: Princeton University Press, 1979.

Psychology

Gallop, Jane. *The Daughter's Seduction: Feminism and Psychoanalysis.* Ithaca: Cornell University Press, 1982.

Gilligan, Carol. *In a Different Voice: Psychological Theory and Women's Development.* Cambridge: Harvard University Press, 1982.

Herman, Judith. *Father-Daughter Incest.* Cambridge: Harvard University Press, 1981.

Maccoby, Eleanor, and Carol Jacklin. *The Psychology of Sex Differences.* Stanford: Stanford University Press, 1974.

Miller, Jean Baker. *Toward a New Psychology of Women.* New York: Beacon Press, 1977.

Mitchell, Juliet. *Psychoanalysis and Feminism.* New York: Random House, 1975.

Parlee, Mary Brown. "Review Essay: Psychology and Women." *Signs* I, 1 (Autumn 1975); and *Signs* V,1 (Autumn 1979).

Religion

Baum, Charlotte Paula Hyman, and Sonya Michel. *The Jewish Woman in America*. New York: Dial Books, 1976.

Daly, Mary. *Beyond God the Father: Toward a Philosophy of Women's Liberation*. New York: Beacon Press, 1973.

Pagels, Elaine. *The Gnostic Gospels*. New York: Random House, 1979.

Ruether, Rosemary Radford. *Religion and Sexism*. New York: Simon & Schuster, 1974.

Science

Haraway, Donna. "Animal Sociology and a Natural Economy of the Body Politic," parts I and II. *Signs* IV, 1 (Autumn 1978). See also the *Signs* special issue on Women and Science, of which this essay is a part.

Rossiter, Margaret. *Women Scientists in America: Struggles and Strategies to 1940*. Baltimore: Johns Hopkins University Press, 1982.

Sexuality and Health

Boston Women's Health Collective. *Our Bodies, Ourselves: A Course by and for Women*. Revised edition. New York: Simon & Schuster, 1976.

Chernin, Kim. *The Obsession: Reflections on the Tyranny of Slenderness*. New York: Harper & Row, 1981.

Ehrenreich, Barbara, and Deirdre English. *For Her Own Good: 150 Years of the Experts' Advice to Women*. New York: Doubleday, 1979.

Petchesky, Rosalind. *Abortion and Woman's Choice: The State, Sexuality, and Reproductive Freedom*. New York: Longman, 1983.

Stimpson, Catharine, and Ethel Person, eds. *Women: Sex and Sexuality*. Chicago: University of Chicago Press, 1981.

Vance, Carole S. *Pleasure and Danger*. London and Boston: Routledge & Kegan Paul, 1984.

Theory

Atkinson, Ti-Grace. *Amazon Odyssey: The First Collection of Writings by the Political Pioneer of the Women's Movement.* New York: Links Books, 1974.

Beauvoir, Simone de. *The Second Sex.* New York: Knopf, 1983.

Brownmiller, Susan. *Against Our Will: Men, Women, and Rape.* New York: Simon & Schuster, 1975.

Bunch, Charlotte. Introduction. *Building Feminist Theory: Essays from Quest.* New York: Longman, 1981.

Donovan, Josephine. *Feminist Theory: The Intellectual Tradition of American Feminism.* New York: Frederick Ungar, 1985.

Eisenstein, Hester, and Alice Jardine, eds. *The Future of Difference.* 1980. Reprint. G.K. Hall, 1985.

Eisenstein, Zillah. *The Radical Future of Liberal Feminism.* New York: Longman, 1980.

Engels, Friedrich. *On the Origin of the Family, Private Property, and the State.* 1884. New York: Pathfinders Printers, 1972.

Firestone, Shulamith. *The Dialectic of Sex: The Case for Feminist Revolution.* New York: Morrow, 1970.

Friedan, Betty. *The Feminine Mystique.* New York: Norton, 1963.

Gilman, Charlotte Perkins. *Women and Economics.* 1898. New York: Harper & Row, 1970.

Gornick, Vivian, and Barbara Moran, eds. *Woman in Sexist Society.* New York: Basic Books, 1971.

Jaggar, Alison, and Paula Rothenberg. *Feminist Frameworks: Alternative Theoretical Accounts of the Relations between Men and Women.* New York: McGraw-Hill, 1977.

Janeway, Elizabeth. *Man's World, Woman's Place.* New York: Morrow, 1971.

Keohane, Nannerl, Michelle Rosaldo, and Barbara C. Gelpi, eds. *Feminist Theory: A Critique of Ideology.* Chicago: University of Chicago Press, 1982.

Koedt, Ann, Ellen Levine, and Anita Rapone, eds. *Radical Feminism.* New York: Times Books, 1973.

Marks, Elaine, and Isabelle de Courtivron, eds. *New French Feminisms.* Amherst: University of Massachusetts Press, 1979.

Mill, John Stuart. *The Subjection of Women.* 1869. Cambridge, Mass.: MIT Press, 1970.

Millett, Kate. *Sexual Politics.* New York: Doubleday, 1970.

Mitchell, Juliet. *Woman's Estate.* New York: Random House, 1973.

Morgan, Robin, ed. *Sisterhood Is Powerful: An Anthology of Writings from the Women's Liberation Movement.* New York: Random House, 1970.

Rowbotham, Sheila. *Woman's Consciousness, Man's World.* New York: Penguin, 1974.

Schecter, Susan. *Women and Male Violence: The Visions and Struggles of the Battered Women's Movement.* Boston: South End Press, 1982.

Third World Women

Davis, Angela Y. *Women, Race and Class.* New York: Random House, 1981.

Green, Rayna. *Native American Women: A Contextual Bibliography.* Bloomington: Indiana University Press, 1983.

Hull, Gloria, Barbara Smith, and Patricia Bell Scott, eds. *But Some of Us Are Brave: Black Women's Studies.* New York: Feminist Press, 1981.

Lerner, Gerda, ed. *Black Women in White America: A Documentary History.* New York: Pantheon, 1972.

Moraga, Cherrié, and Gloria Anzaldúa. *This Bridge Called My Back: Writings by Radical Women of Color.* Watertown, Mass.: Persephone Press, 1982.

Smith, Barbara, ed. *Home Girls: A Black Feminist Anthology.* New York: Kitchen Table, 1983.

Washington, Mary Helen, ed. *Black-Eyed Susans: Classic Stories by and about Black Women.* New York: Doubleday, 1975.

———. *Midnight Birds: Stories of Contemporary Black Women Writers.* New York: Doubleday, 1980.

Women's Studies and Education

Abel, Elizabeth, and Emily K. Abel. *The Signs Reader: Women, Gender and Scholarship.* Chicago: University of Chicago Press, 1983.

Ballou, Patricia. *Women: A Bibliography of Bibliographies.* New York: G.K. Hall & Co., 1980.

Boxer, Marilyn. "For and about Women: The Theory and Practice of Women's Studies in the United States." *Signs* 7, 3 (Spring 1982).

Cruikshank, Margaret, ed. *Lesbian Studies.* New York: Feminist Press, 1982.

Graham, Patricia Albjerg. "Expansion and Exclusion: A History of Women in American Higher Education." *Signs* III, 4 (Summer 1978).

76

Howe, Florence. *Myths of Coeducation: Selected Essays 1964-1983.* Bloomington: Indiana University Press, 1984.

———. *Seven Years Later: Women's Studies Programs in 1976.* Washington, D.C.: National Advisory Council on Women's Educational Programs, 1977.

Hunter College, Women's Studies Collective. *Women's Realities, Women's Choices: An Introduction to Women's Studies.* New York: Oxford University Press, 1983.

Rossi, Alice, and Ann Calderwood, eds. *Academic Women on the Move.* New York: Russell Sage, 1973.

Stineman, Esther. *Women's Studies: A Recommended Core Bibliography.* Littleton, Conn.: Libraries Unlimited, 1979.

Women's Studies Quarterly. 10 (Spring 1982). "A Special Feature: Transforming the Curriculum."

Zak, Michele, and Patricia Moots. *Women and the Politics of Culture.* New York: Longman, 1983.